Eric

Trust Logue will also enjoy this after you have finished!

Cheers

George

Dec 2003

One Dog an

One Dog and His Man

One Dog and His Man

NOTES FROM AN ALL-WEATHER WALKER

Trevor Grove

Illustrated by Posy Simmonds

Atlantic Books
London

First published in
Great Britain in 2003
by Atlantic Books,
an imprint of
Grove Atlantic Ltd.

1 3 5 7 9 8 6 4 2

A CIP catalogue record for this book
is available from the British Library.

1 84354 179 3

Printed by Mackays of Chatham Ltd

Atlantic Books
An imprint of Grove Atlantic Ltd
Ormond House
26–27 Boswell Street
London
WC1N 3JZ

Contents

OCTOBER	The Dawn Patrol	1
NOVEMBER	Territorial Imperatives	13
DECEMBER	Tooth and Claw	23
JANUARY	Meeting and Greeting	35
FEBRUARY	Matters of Breeding	45
MARCH	Dogs of Renown	63
APRIL	Performing Dogs	77
MAY – JUNE – JULY	A Dog Down Under	93
AUGUST	Agony and Ecstasy	101
SEPTEMBER	Tail Piece	114
	A Word From His Mistress	116
	Some Books About Dogs	119
	Acknowledgements	121

The Dawn Patrol

It is 7.30 on the first autumn morning that's been cold enough for gloves. The dog and I have the Heath to ourselves, all 791 acres of it. There is a dusting of frost on the slope leading down to the lake, where a pair of swans glide through the mist like phantom schooners. Below us, across the roofs of Holloway and Islington, alarm clocks are going off and London is rousing itself, as the sun inches wanly above the skyline.

> This City now doth, like a garment, wear
> The beauty of the morning; silent, bare,
> Ships, towers, domes, theatres, and temples lie
> Open unto the fields, and to the sky.

Here on Hampstead Heath, overlooking the waking capital, are the only fields left that Wordsworth would recognize as such. A whiff of woodsmoke is in the air. There are rabbit tracks in the frozen grass by the lake's edge and a kestrel is hunting overhead.

I take a deep, cold breath and think, God's in his heaven – all's right with the world.

The dog sniffs and thinks, Dog's in his heaven – and blow me if someone hasn't dropped a cheese sandwich under that bench.

This pretty well sums up our different attitudes to our daily walk. For me the pluses are exercise, communing with nature, and an hour to listen to the radio or a talking book. Like an authentic countryman, I don't forget to salute any magpies I see with a muttered 'Good day' to ward off bad luck, though I don't always spit and raise my hat, as one's supposed to.

For the dog, once the most basic functions have been seen to, the principal charm of walking is the opportunity for illicit food and sex. Never mind that his scavenging is seldom successful and his courtships are never consummated. It is a case of travelling hopefully, which he does with a springy optimism absolutely undimmed by disappointment. Every dog has his day, we say. And *this* is the day, says the dog, as he torpedoes out of the car door each morning, bursting with anticipation (unlike the morose mutt in a *New Yorker* cartoon by James Stevenson who says gloomily, 'Speaking personally, I haven't had my day, and I've never met any dog who has').

So this walking business is an example of what one might

call therapeutic symbiosis. I need the dog to give a kick-start and focus to my daily life. The dog needs me to escort him to wide open spaces where he can give vent to his feverish instincts as hunter and Lothario.

What we have in common, the dog and I, is that we are seldom happier than when we are thus engaged. We have been at it for eight years, with barely a morning missed. Very occasionally, when the alarm goes off and it's still dark outside, I baulk at the invariable routine. 'What about a film called *Hound-dog Day*?' I mutter from beneath the duvet, as the dog tears into the bedroom and nibbles my toes by way of inducement. But once we are out in the open, resentment vanishes. We know every ditch and tree-stump of the Heath, every glade and litter-bin of adjoining Kenwood. This is the oak on whose trunk a scarlet beef-steak mushroom grows each autumn – if I can get there before the Italian fungus-lovers pounce. And here are the best-cropping blackberry bushes in the whole of London. The dog has his own Michelin-starred venues worth a detour: the back-door of the café kitchen; the hollow in the beech tree roots where he can always find a drink of scummy water.

He covers four or five miles twice a day – come rain or shine, snow or heat-wave – once with me, once with his mistress. We are properly equipped. My stout waterproof boots are by Chris Brasher, my waterproof hat by someone called Simon Fairfax, my audio-tape courtesy of The Talking Book Club. I have a pocketful of bone-shaped biscuits called Gravybones to maintain discipline and a knobbly stick in case of dog-fights. The dog doesn't care for hail or heavy downpours, so on stormy days he slips on a rugged canvas coat called a Dryzabone, made in Australia, which makes him look like a canine member of the Ned Kelly gang.

If you are a shepherd or a shooter or an Antarctic explorer, the dogs in your life have an obvious role and purpose. In my own case, I think that if dogs didn't need walking, one might as well have a cat.

Dogs are so dependably loving, people say. I mean people who like dogs, of course. They include some pretty thoughtful types, Elizabeth Barrett Browning and Sigmund Freud, for instance, Rudyard Kipling and Jilly Cooper, not to mention Charlie Brown and T.S. Eliot. The author of *Old Possum's Book of Practical Cats*, reborn as *Cats*, the musical's answer to *The Mousetrap*, was really a dog person, according to his widow. He once wrote an elegy to a Yorkshire terrier.

This is how Siegfried Sassoon (1886–1967) described the relationship in his poem 'Man and Dog':

Who's this – alone with stone and sky?
It's only my old dog and I –
It's only him; it's only me;
Alone with stone and grass and tree.

What share we most – we two together?
Smells, and awareness of the weather.
What is it makes us more than dust?
My trust in him; in me his trust.

Here's anyhow one decent thing
That life to man and dog can bring;
One decent thing, remultiplied
Till earth's last dog and man have died.

I say that dogs are, at best, not so much dependably loving as lovably dependent. At worst, they are simply parasites. According to authorities on this matter, most of the 400,000,000 dogs in the world fall into the latter category. They are scavengers, living on the edge of poor villages, unwanted and unloved but thriving nonetheless. The fortunate minority are not only thriving, but loved and wanted, too. This does not stop them being scavengers.

Man's best friend would sell you down the river for a stale bun or a dead hedgehog. Small boys dream of having a four-legged chum like Snoopy or William Brown's Jumble. Grown-ups know that on close acquaintance a dog is not so much a friend as a dim-witted but wilful foster-child. If it is beautiful it wins your admiration; if it is good-natured and amusing, your aVection; if none of the above, well then, your resentful tolerance. And that's about it. Lassie and Greyfriars Bobby are special cases. Nana, the Darling family's Newfoundland nurse in *Peter Pan*, is an impossible dream. No human nanny could match such uncomplaining devotion.

Border collies, with their desperate obsession to please their masters and round up anything that moves, are genetic one-offs, as summed up in a wonderful Gary Larson cartoon. It shows a flock of bewildered-looking sheep attempting to have a social gathering. A sheepdog has just rung the doorbell. The host sheep is saying, 'This party's chaos. Nobody knows where to stand. Oh, thank God, here comes a border collie.'

The understanding between my own dog and myself is very limited. If I were out walking with a human companion and said, 'Hey, come and have a look at this', he'd either ask me what it was or amble over, showing signs of curiosity and interest. But this dog, my supposed chum, is seldom so obliging. Bidden to come over, he will shoot a look at me – a look of pure, instant calculation. There is only one question to be read in his eyes and that is, 'If I do, what's in it for me?' Is there some sort of reward to be had? Or will he be better off carrying on what he was doing before the interruption?

Mostly he chooses the latter option. He adopts the baffled look of a Kensington matron approached in the street by a beggar. He pretends not to understand and just keeps going. So much for unconditional love.

Dog books tell you that Dalmatians, as a breed, are prone to deafness. This is true. But they make no mention of the selective version of the affliction, which is what affects my Dalmatian. His normal hearing is supernatural by human standards. Even asleep, he will detect someone scraping out the last of the Marmite jar in the kitchen four floors below and thunder downstairs to lick it clean. He can hear the car engine being switched off a block away. This is the signal to leap on to the sofa and press his muzzle against the window, adding to the pattern of smeary noseprints on the glass.

But when it comes to less welcome sounds, such as a frantic 'Come here!' when night is falling and the park gates are about to close, he simply twists the volume control to zero. He has perfected a blank look, which appears to mean, 'Who? Me? I'm a touch hard of hearing, you know.'

'Read my lips,' I snarl. But he just slopes off with a shrug, wagging his tail.

He has a similar problem with his eyesight. Generally speaking, it is exceptionally keen. He can spot a crumpled crisp packet at a hundred yards with the precision of a buzzard. But there are moments when a strange blindness overtakes him. He waves his head about pathetically, as if trying to make out where you are, when all the time you're shouting, waving your hat and jumping up and down like a castaway hailing a passing ship.

It is that time of year when there is a threat of winter in the slate sky, but autumn has not yet given up the blighted struggle to give Londoners a taste of mists and mellow fruitfulness. What we get instead is mud and drooping leaflessness. That frosty morning was just a tease. The days get shorter, but there is no compensating sparkle in the air. The effect is unsettling.

For the past week the dog has been transformed into a sex-fiend. On his second walk of the day, at lunchtime, he's off like a fire-and-forget missile, tripping joggers and scattering toddlers en route. I whistle commandingly as he rockets up Parliament Hill. He affects not to hear, and vanishes over the brow in the general direction of St Paul's Cathedral.

Fifteen minutes later he flashes past, heading the other way – tail up, snout down, legs going like scissors. 'Biscuits!' I shout, and put my hand in my pocket. This generally works better than the command 'Heel!' (To be truthful, the command 'Heel!' scarcely works at all, despite the fact that we have a handsome blue graduation certificate from Mr Uncle, the North London dog-trainer. We do a masterly 'Sit!' but not in mid-gallop, unfortunately.)

'Biscuits,' I implore. But all I get is a 20mph toss of the head. Black spots and white fur merge into a single dot and vanish northwards.

This sexual obsessiveness is a bit of a mystery, given the time of year. Other owners of male dogs are experiencing the same phenomenon. We have been exchanging notes, watching our charges criss-cross the meadow like mine-sweepers. The wet grass must be heaving with come-hitherish hormones. We expect some friskiness in the spring. But what's with this autumn bacchanal? Have all the bitches in North London suddenly come on heat together? Is this a final fling of synchronized seduction before winter sets in?

Beezle – that's the Dalmatian's name – disappeared for a full half-hour this morning. The conventional wisdom among dog-walkers is that you don't go searching about after a straying pooch. You stay put, calling out like a fog-horn at intervals, and trust the truant will eventually retrace his or her steps. In due course, just as visions of a deranged dog haring along the North Circular were beginning to trouble me, Beezle reappeared over the horizon with his nose clamped to the rear end of a spaniel. She was a miserable, bow-legged creature. If she'd been human you'd have called her a dog. But she plainly had something. Beezle was prancing along behind her behind as though on springs.

The spaniel was on a lead, being tugged forwards by a man with a Basil Fawlty moustache and an escort of small children. He looked furious.

'Is this your dog?' he barked.

'Yes,' I said.

'Well, why can't you damn well keep him under control? He's been pestering my bitch for the last half an hour. Won't let her alone. Very awkward with all these children.'

The children nudged each other knowingly.

I knew who was the injured party in this instance. 'Look,' I said indignantly, ungluing Beezle from the spaniel's tail-end and putting the lead on him, 'if anyone's to blame it's you. Your dog's either in season or about to be or just has been. She's been laying a trail all over the bloody Heath, maddening every male for miles around. You shouldn't bring her out in that state.'

Instead of apologizing, the man glared at me. Was I about to witness an outbreak of dog rage? 'As a matter of

fact,' he said, spitting out the words like hot rivets, 'she's been spayed.'

We retreated, shame-faced. Admittedly Beezle's a virgin. At any rate, I think he is. Even so, judging by his generally cocky manner, I'd always taken it for granted that when it came to sniffing out talent he was as reliable as Warren Beatty. This was a blow to his machismo and, by extension, mine. As we know, the self-esteem of dog-owners is closely linked with that of their dogs.

Later, it occurred to me that the man had been lying. Judging by his blimpish manner, he was probably in denial. I've noticed before that the owners of bitches caught out in this way react with a sort of defensive hostility, as though their pet's powers of sexual enslavement were no one's business but their own.

In human terms, it would be like leading a naked Page Three girl into a rugby club and then accusing the oglers of harassment.

Territorial Imperatives

The autumn gales have swept the Heath clean of the smell of sex. Beezle is still led by his nose on our daily walk, but the search is no longer so frenzied. He is back to his normal, simple pleasures: trotting nowhere in particular; wagging or growling at acquaintances; barking at tramps and winos and anyone carrying an oddly shaped package or wearing almost any kind of hat. He also gets frantic if he sees a couple dancing, though this is unusual on the Heath. Fortunately he has grown out of barking at black people. This is just as well. I never knew whether it made things better or worse to apologize.

Above all he likes peeing on things. His bladder is never on empty. Quite unlike humans, he positively hoards his urine, rationing it out in tiny squirts. A Coke tin, a toadstool, the roots of an ancient oak that has stood there since America was still a colony, every object in his path earns rapt attention. He does not discriminate. The interest is not in the thing observed, unless it is edible, but in letting the world know that it has *been* observed, and marked, *by him*.

Urino ergo sum. He will make a beeline through a clump of thistles solely to cock his leg on a fresh molehill. He'll risk death to have a tinkle on a throbbing tractor tyre. Such are a dog's mysterious drives.

In Stephen Budiansky's eye-opening book, *The Truth About Dogs*, I learn that this thoroughly offensive method of marking territory is inherited from wolves:

> The primary stimulus for raised-leg urination
> in wolves is not, as is often said, the smell of a
> strange wolf's urine but rather the presence of
> the wolf's *own* mark: there is a strong instinct to
> mark and remark sites along frequently travelled
> routes within the wolf's own territory.

A contingent theory is that dogs are not only marking their own patches but also eliminating the traces of rivals. *The Hidden Life of Dogs* is a beguiling account by the American writer Elizabeth Marshall Thomas of her family of huskies in Cambridge, Massachusetts. After a heavy snowfall, she noticed that Misha, the top dog or alpha-male in the household, would not only pee where other dogs had left their marks, which were yellowishly visible in the snow, but, if necessary, would treat them to several repeated wettings until the other stain had been entirely obliterated by his own. She also observed Misha's curious habit of trying to place his marks as high as possible. He would twist his belly skywards and almost dislocate his rear leg in order to do so. She decided he was hoping to give the impression that he was actually a much taller dog than he really was, as if the Hound of the Baskervilles had lately passed by.

(Perhaps a combination of such instincts is at work in the brains of urban graffiti-artists, which would explain why a single graffito always stimulates others, until a once-pristine patch of wall is covered in a tangle of intertwining tags.)

There is a thick bank of fog over the ponds. The squirrels are out and about. For months during the summer they seemed to have disappeared. I can make out no pattern to their behaviour. In days past, when everything was as God intended, squirrels gambolled around during the warm seasons of the year, gathered nuts in the autumn, and hibernated all winter. In London they no longer seem to be governed by traditional timetables, any more than our children are. Just as teenagers think nothing of treating night

as day – staying out till six in the morning, not rising until *Neighbours* – modern squirrels have forgotten their old bed-times. You find them larking about in February frosts. One morning, when the ponds were frozen over, I even saw one skating, his little arms aloft, tail braced, as he mistook the ice for terra firma.

This unseasonal behaviour must be another consequence of global warming, on top of which London is already noticeably overheated compared with the country-side. Autumn lasts until mid-December. Daffodils and rhododendrons bloom in March, sometimes sooner. Life has become soft, the litter-bins bulge and there's no longer the need to spend the shortening days stocking the larder for lean times ahead. If this goes on, whatever will become of the squirrel as a symbol of the prudent building-society saver?

When he was younger Beezle was an enthusiastic squirrel hunter. But after hundreds of fruitless pursuits which ended with him splatting into a tree-trunk like a cartoon character, he learned wisdom. Nowadays, at the great age

of eight, he'll only give chase if the quarry is out in the open, well away from aerial escape routes. It must be a sign of canine cunning that whenever he does spot a foolish young squirrel in such circumstances, he no longer aims at the creature itself but races directly towards the nearest tree, knowing this is where it will make for. But still, no dice. Just as he's about to cut it off at the pass, the artful dodger jinks, leaps, and hits the bark just ahead of the bite, before scampering aloft.

Beezle has drawn blood only twice in his life. The first time was on a May morning when he caught a baby rabbit in Kenwood. He was so startled he simply stared as it lay panting on the ground, like an urban motorist who's run over a pheasant on a country lane. I had to finish it off. I was unsure whether to be proud of the dog's hunting skill, or ashamed that he'd picked on such a juvenile. My previous Dalmatian, Gus, once caught a rabbit when we were walking by the Thames near Goring. But it was a full-grown buck and we expiated the shame by eating the victim. I made a fire and cooked it, Boy Scout fashion, on a stick. Then Gus and I shared the stringy prize. We felt at one with nature. The experience was slightly marred by the lack of salt.

Beezle's other catch was a rat. North London gardens are lifting with urbanized wildlife, including foxes, owls and squadrons of magpies, the ethnic cleansers of the bird-world.

The rats are less visible, but we know they're there because Smoky the cat used to bring their bloody heads into the house, Salome fashion, and leave them on the children's beds as love tokens. The one Beezle pounced on couldn't have been very streetwise. It went foraging in the compost heap in broad daylight. It died instantly, at which point the hunter lost interest and lay down in the sun beside the corpse – very uncatlike behaviour.

The urban fox has been commonplace in London since the early 1970s. I once saw the body of a fine, russet-furred male lying in the gutter just outside the Wren church where my wife and I were married, St Vedast's, just a few steps from St Paul's, in the very heart of the City. Last spring a pair of cubs spent their mornings playing at the bottom of our garden. When they weren't playing they were scratching, since they were both horribly mangy. Beezle never seemed to pick up their scent; no hound genes there, one gathered. Had he done so, what would his reaction have been? The Beaufort pack may know instinctively that any member of the genus *Vulpes* must be torn to shreds on sight. But were Beezle, metropolitan in tooth and claw, to meet Reynard face to face, it's more likely he would simply assume he was encountering another, rather pongy, dog.

After all, there's at least as strong a family resemblance between a Dalmatian and a fox as between a chow and a chihuahua. It has often struck me as extraordinary that different breeds of dog recognize each other for what they are. Introduce a Rottweiler to a Yorkie for the first time and you might think the tabloid terror-dog would take the tiny terrier for a canapé. In fact, they are much more likely to sniff each other's bottoms. In the right circumstances they'll even try to mate.

This is bizarre, if you think about it. The rest of the animal kingdom doesn't go in for surprises of this kind. It is as if an elephant belonged to the same species as an anteater, or a great white shark made friends with an anchovy.

So Beezle's never seen a fox, even when we almost bumped into a magnificent bushy-brushed specimen one dewy summer dawn on the Heath. 'Look,' I whispered in David Attenborough *sotto voce*, nudging Beezle with my knee. 'Over there.' It stood stock-still staring at us for a few seconds, silhouetted against the rising sun, before loping back into the undergrowth. But Beezle had one of his sudden attacks of blindness and focused his attention on a passing bee.

A while later the lives of dog and fox became entwined willy-nilly, with disagreeable results. Beezle began to scratch and fret like the tormented protagonist of Kipling's *How The Rhinoceros Got His Skin*. He couldn't sit still for a second. His back legs jigged like pistons. He tore at himself with his claws. Scabs appeared on his head. In line with the great conspiracy to put vets' fees on a par with Harley Street, a blood sample was sent off for analysis – to Stockholm. As we awaited the results, fellow dog-walkers with experience of country living offered a swifter diagnosis: fox mange. The Swedish lab eventually and expensively confirmed this. The cubs at the bottom of our garden had dropped the eggs, larvae, mites or whatever they were, into the grass and the dog had picked them up. Now they were breeding and feeding and generally gadding about beneath his skin and driving him mad. A bath in a deadly chemical probably banned by the World Health Organization finally wrought a cure, but not before I'd come to wish we had a Highgate and Crouch End Hunt to carry out a spot of cubbing in the area.

A couple of mornings ago my wife called to me excitedly. In the next-door garden a full-grown gentleman fox had settled himself down for a sun-bathe. He was lounging in a deck-chair left out there since the summer, with his legs crossed, looking as cool as you please. Unless my eyes deceived me, he was smoking a cheroot.

DECEMBER
Tooth and Claw

Beezle's full name is Beesley, which needs explaining. In 1996 my wife published a biography of Dodie Smith, the playwright and novelist best-known for her immortal classic *The Hundred and One Dalmatians*. As Valerie did her research, she became infected by Dodie's besottedness with spotted dogs.

'I began to feel, as Dodie did, that a house without a dog was incomplete,' she wrote in her foreword.

> The moment I had finished my manuscript,
> one Sunday evening in November, I rang the
> British Dalmatian Club and asked whether there
> were any litters near London at the moment.
> There were three; the nearest was in Welwyn
> Garden City. I rang the breeder, who told me
> that from a litter of nine with the finest of
> pedigrees, only one was still unspoken for –
> 'a dear little boy'.

Unknown to me, whose Christmas present he was to be, the dear little boy had already been named. Had he been a bitch, he'd have been Dodie, naturally. As things were, it was pre-ordained that he should be called after Dodie's husband, the good-natured Alec Beesley, who had first met Dodie in the 1930s before she became famous, when both of them worked at Heal's department store on Tottenham Court Road.

> Five days later [Valerie wrote] my eldest daughter and I drove up in the December dawn to collect 'Mr Beesley'. He now occupies a central role in our household. Apart from being the handsomest dog in the world, he seems to me to embody the spirit and *joie de vivre* of the Dalmatian at its best.

Of the many Dalmatians she cherished, Dodie's favourite was called Buzzle. So it was inevitable that Mr Beesley, a scrap of spotty fur barely distinguishable from the hot-water-bottle covers Boots were selling that winter, became Beezle. (Scholars of canine nomenclature will be interested to know that my previous, pre-marriage Dalmatian, the rabbit-killer Gus, was often known as Goozle.)

This account will be irrelevant to any child under ten. For them, thanks to Dodie and Disney, all Dalmatians are called

24

Pongo, whatever their sex. Dalmatian-owners fight this tendency as best they can with ingenious names such as Domino and Dot, but it does no good. You might as well try calling a baby elephant something other than Dumbo.

'Look, there's one of those spotted dogs,' simper the mothers.

'It's Pongo!' squeal their video-literate children.

One cleverer-than-usual moppet was taken aback when I told her the name was not Pongo but Beezle. She considered his spots thoughtfully for a moment, then looked up with a smile of keen intelligence. 'Oh, I see,' she said. 'Measle. That's a good name for him.'

And it was, rather.

Beezle arrived cradled in my eldest daughter's arms. He was wrapped in a towel, slimy with car-sick and utterly woebegone. He was about the size of a two-pound bag of sugar and just as sweet, as all baby things are apart from moles and mice. For the first few weeks of their lives Dalmatian puppies are pure white. Then their spots begin to show, like a sprinkling of soot. Beezle had a heart-shaped one on the left-hand side of his nose. I found the smell of his infant sick inoffensive, as only parents do. Nature's bonding mechanism was at work.

I am not sentimental about dogs in general. As a genus, they are despicable in all sorts of ways. They have vile habits, small brains, gross appetites and a limited range of uses. Yet when a newspaper editor once commissioned me to write an article about being a dog-owner in London and changed the pronoun 'he' to 'it' throughout the article I was livid. 'It and I went for a walk in Kensington Gardens' not only had an unfeeling ring about it but completely mis-represented the bond between man and dog – or man and canary, come to that.

One does not 'own' a domestic animal in the same way that one owns a bicycle or a geranium. Acknowledgement of gender is just one of the differences. There is a contrac-tual aspect to the relationship, an element of give and take, even if it's pretty unbalanced: a winning racehorse or a good gun-dog gives more than it takes, I presume, whereas your average tortoise offers almost no return on the lettuce leaves invested.

The awful fate of Tommy, the tortoise I had as a small boy, demonstrates that, even in the infant human mind, this contract is a reality. However much I tempted him with celery and carrot sticks, Tommy always refused to poke his head out when friends came to call. One day, driven to drastic measures by his uncooperativeness, I took a pair of sugar tongs to his withdrawn head, wielding them like an obstetrician's forceps. The result was traumatic and terminal.

Pet-owners must get used to a certain amount of nature

in the raw. Our Burmese cat was a ruthless murderer, hauling corpses of various kinds into the house throughout his hunting years. The hamsters never lasted long. Despite stringent precautions, Smoky awaited his chances with unblinking patience and did for all of them sooner or later. He once slaughtered a pair of the miniature Russian variety on the bed in our guest room. My brother was asleep in it at the time and woke to find his chest covered in blood and fur.

A pet rabbit, Sticky Bun, also died on the premises. The case remains unsolved. We returned from a day out to find the hutch had been ram-raided, the door torn open and the poor little creature lifeless on the floor. There were no marks on her, so it was a matter of tearful debate whether Sticky Bun's neck had been broken or whether she had simply died of fright. Beezle and Smoky looked (if one can use the expression about a dog and a cat) equally sheepish. The jury divided on cat versus dog lines and to this day has not reached a verdict. Could it have been a team effort?

The incident reminds me of a favourite urban myth. Two families lived next door to each other. One had a dog, the other a beautiful angora rabbit, housed in a hutch in the garden. One evening, to his horror, the paterfamilias of the former household discovered his dog holding the dead rabbit in its jaws. Mortified and guilt-stricken, he shampooed the corpse, blow-dried it and then, creeping through the hedge in the early hours of the morning, replaced it in its hutch, artfully arranging the body so that the neighbours would think it had died in its sleep.

A day or two passed. The dog-owner, driven by curiosity, asked his neighbour how the rabbit was doing.

'Funny you should ask,' said the other, looking strangely disturbed. 'The oddest thing happened. Our rabbit died last week – it was quite old, you know – and we buried it in the garden. The children held a funeral service. Put a cross on the grave and so on. Then the day before yesterday, the kids came screaming into the house to say the rabbit was alive again. Well, it wasn't, actually. But there it was, back in its hutch, looking as clean and fluffy as though it had risen from the dead. It's absolutely inexplicable.'

Beezle carries the scars of several bloody encounters with other dogs. Ironically, the worst of them occurred as a direct result of Dodie Smith. Some scenes in the remake of *The Hundred and One Dalmatians* – the version that used real animals and live human actors, led by Glenn Close as Cruella – were shot just near Kenwood House. Naturally, this being a film, the setting didn't look natural enough, so a small wooded hill was sprayed with tons of stuff that looked like shaving foam to create a snowy winter scene. Beezle and I stood at the edge of the shaving foam one

afternoon to watch the doggy stars going through their paces.

I was transfixed. Here were two Dalmatians – Dalmatians! – behaving like border collies in *One Man and His Dog*. Ignoring the milling throng of best boys and grips and assistant producers talking into mobiles, they went hither and yon, sat, lay, rolled in the fake snow, looked inquisitive … all at the command of a young man in jeans who barely raised his voice above a whisper.

Beezle yawned distractedly and made off towards a tray of buns on the ground next to the camera crew. I called him back, panicking slightly, and was so impressed when he obeyed that I gave him a biscuit. There was a yell from a young woman with a clipboard who goose-stepped over to us.

'Hey, you! Don't you *dare* feed that dog,' she bawled.

'But it's my dog,' I stammered.

'Whaddyamean, your dog?'

'He's my dog and we were just watching the filming.'

'You sure it's not one of the cast?'

'Quite sure,' I said. But we were ordered off the set all the same. We left with our tails between our legs. At least they might have offered Beezle a trot-on part as an extra, I thought. How could they fail to be struck by his great handsomeness? He had a heart-shaped spot on his nose, after all. Whereas we'd seen Pongo *being made-up*.

The chance to recover some pride after this humiliating scene offered itself a few months later when the movie was released. Our local paper, the *Hampstead and Highgate Express*, better-known as the *Ham and High*, decided to organize a photo-call of local Dalmatians to mark the occasion. About a dozen dogs and their owners, including Beezle and his mistress, showed up at Kenwood House for the shoot. They swaggered about, disrupted the photographer's attempts to pose them and became generally over-excited. That was when Duke and Danny, two muscular dogs, who had always struck me as being on the brutish side, suddenly turned on Beezle in a frenzy and began tearing lumps out of him. A scene of terrible carnage ensued.

I had a frantic call from my wife and drove to Kenwood like the wind, bearing TCP and bandages. Beezle was in a shocking state, on his feet, but covered in blood, trembling uncontrollably.

The South African vet was appalled. 'I saw a dog as badly wounded as this once, but he'd been mauled by a lion.' Which was another way of saying the bill would be well over £500.

There were, I think, seven deep bites, two down to the bone. There was a lot of stitching to be done. Yet by the time we collected him a few hours later, covered in shaved patches painted over with scarlet Hibiscrub, he was as perky as could be.

Not for the last time, I was struck by the astonishing resilience of dogs, which no doubt applies to other animals too. Perhaps such swift powers of recovery account for the cruelties men have inflicted on their fellow creatures in the past – bear-baiting, cock-fights, goats and donkeys dropped off Spanish church-towers and the like – without their consciences being troubled. But that isn't to say the memory doesn't linger. Beezle never forgot Duke and Danny, who, after this first blooding, went on to terrorize the dog-walkers of Hampstead Heath and Kenwood for months until they were sentenced first to castration, then exiled altogether. Since then, he approaches any male Dalmatian in a state of high alert, as though walking on stilts, ready to fight or fly, but more probably fly.

City dogs tend to be far more socialized than their country cousins, so long as they aren't forced to be kept on leads all the time by ignorant and bossy by-laws. They can't afford to be territorial since outside their own yards and gardens the territory is shared. City-dwelling humans show similar tolerance, putting up with the enforced intimacies of a rush-hour Tube train that would be intolerable in any other circumstances. Nevertheless, Beezle has his enemies, notably a large, handsome Alsatian called Wagner.

The interestingly named Wagner, who might possibly have turned out differently had he been called Mozart or Liszt, has lately been forced to wear a muzzle, as a result of mounting complaints to the park police. Before, the fear of a chance meeting haunted quite a few of us, which is why I took to carrying a knobbly stick. Wagner attacked Beezle more than once. On the last occasion, the wound was deep enough for me to get most of my thumb into it. Even now that he is (usually) muzzled he is still prone to knock dogs over. I watched him set upon a black Labrador only the other day. The latter's beefy American owner jumped on to the wrestling dogs and spreadeagled himself on top of them until Wagner had calmed down.

That's my worry about Alsatians, or German shepherds, if you prefer. They are usually so disciplined. But when they break out, it's like releasing a tightly coiled spring.

'It's the pub dogs you want to watch out for,' warned a Kenwood friend. 'Stuck behind the bar all week on guard duty. Then they're let out at weekends and they go crazy.'

Apart from his wariness of other Dalmatians, Beezle

appears to be non-racist. He has nothing against Alsatians in general – one of them, Juno, is a puppyhood friend – or any other breed for that matter. Apart from Wagner, his only other sworn enemy is a golden retriever called Taz. The hatred is mutual, and although Taz looks very much like any other retriever to my eyes, these two can spot each other half a mile away. Both of them will stop and narrow their eyes like gunslingers in a cowboy movie. The space between them is instantly transformed into a canine no man's land, across which neither dog will advance but from which neither will retreat, until pressure from UN peacekeepers gives them a decent excuse to quit the field. Even so, the first one to turn away is a cissy.

Meeting and Greeting

Urban dogs have their own strict code of behaviour towards each other. In the wolf pack, everything from sex to dining arrangements hinges on status, ensuring that the alphas dominate. Inter-dog relations are likewise all about rank, though to no practical purpose. Broadly speaking, little dogs (Jack Russells excepted) lower their heads and tails meekly and even throw themselves on to their backs like doormats when confronting big dogs; big dogs submit to even bigger ones. The coolest encounter is simply a rigid-legged stalk-past, staring straight ahead, sometimes accompanied by a curl of the lip and an Al Pacino growl out of the corner of the mouth. ('Hey, buddy, you lookin' at *me*?') This is common among dogs of matching size who are strangers to one another and want to go on believing they are each top dog.

At the friendlier end of the scale is the full *soixante-neuf* bottom-sniffing routine. Things seldom get matier than that unless sex enters the frame, which is almost always, in my dog's case, the result of a misunderstanding. On rare occasions, a younger dog will persuade Beezle to join in a bout of chasing and tumbling, but on the whole he stands on his dignity and won't play. He is, after all, middle-aged in the dog scheme of things. He has lately moved from 'maintenance' food pellets to the 'senior' variety, which can't exactly encourage juvenile larking about. If he were human he'd be getting brochures for Saga cruises in the mail.

There is a parallel etiquette for us walkers. Up until 8.30 a.m., we greet each other warmly with a fulsome 'Good morning. Isn't it a lovely/beastly/utterly vile day?' Those of us listening to the BBC *Today* programme on our Walkmen might even exchange a pithy comment about the morning's news. We recognize each other through the January darkness as members of the Fellowship of the Dawn Dogwalk, particularly in bad weather, and salute each other's hardiness.

This bond of shared intrepidity can lead to life-long friendships. Some thirty years ago I used to walk my previous Dalmatian, Gus, in Kensington Gardens. Gus grew chummy with an Afghan called Jason and I grew chummy with Jason's owners. We would meet at the Round Pond and stroll down to the Serpentine together before breakfast. The consequence was that I became their son's godfather, or perhaps that should be dogfather. Julian is now making his way in the film business, so naturally I advise him to reflect on the number of successful movies with the word 'dog' in the title, such as *Dog Day Afternoon*, *Straw Dogs*, and *Reservoir Dogs*. My suggestion is that *Round Pond Dogs* would have an appealingly non-violent ring to it.

From 8.30 a.m. until *The Archers* at 2 p.m., greetings on the Heath are a little gruffer. A 'hi' or 'hello' or merely a grunt will do. After that, when non-dog people are in the ascendant, there is no acknowledgement whatsoever, unless the oncoming person is walking a dog of the same breed as one's own. This is always a social ice-breaker and will lead to a few minutes of dog-talk about the virtues and vices of the breed, the diseases to which it is prone, the scandalous cost of vets' fees, and so on, while all the time you've got a minimalist dog-show running in your head to decide which of the pair is the finer specimen. In the case of Dalmatians, spotting the winner is easy, since it's all about the marking (that's two puns in one sentence). Shapeliness comes into it too. A fat Dalmatian is the pits, surely the reason that disgusting suety pudding we had at school was called spotted dog.

My brother, who lives in Vancouver, is appalled by the unfriendliness of English dog-walkers. Considerate Canadians not only regard it as good manners to castrate all male dogs as a matter of course, and to poop-scoop even in woods where bears shit unconcernedly; they also feel the

need to greet all other walkers with a 'hi there, howya doing?' and a maple-syrup grin, whatever the time of day. When my brother visits London and tries this on the Heath after the 8.30 a.m. watershed people look at him in alarm.

Celebrities are a special case. Everyone felt happy about hailing the veteran Labour politician Michael Foot in the days when he regularly shambled across the Heath with his dog Dizzy (after Disraeli). He'd hail right back, twirling his stick above his head, his white hair flying.

We always wave at Michael Palin, Python, TV traveller, and jogger extraordinary. I say extraordinary because of his unique, flat-footed running style, which makes one think of a long-legged penguin being pursued by a polar bear. Sometimes he stops for a pant and a chat, before setting off grimly once again, as if a posse of autograph hunters or a personal trainer were close behind him. There is a gang of women joggers who shout, 'We love you, Michael!' when they see him.

A near-contemporary of Michael's, though a Cambridge man, is Bill Oddie, ex-Goodie and birdwatcher. Oddie's website describes itself as 'The unofficial home of the Great Birding One'. The GBO is often to be seen at sunrise standing on the pinnacle of Parliament Hill with his binoculars around his neck. In fact, Beezle and I never dare approach because of his intent look as he scans the heavens with wild surmise, like stout Cortez (who was also bearded), silent, upon a peak in Darien.

It is always tricky, in such a private-cum-public setting as the Heath, to decide whether the famous are mortified to be recognized or even more mortified not to be. I've let my golden chances pass me by more than once. Over the years I have seen Emma Thompson and Kenneth Branagh together; the lovely Emma Thompson alone; new mamma Thompson with baby Gaia in a chic three-wheeled buggy, and on each occasion have managed no more than a low moan of admiration. I have had several sightings of Victoria Wood striding along in a tracksuit, looking determinedly unapproachable. I would have liked to give her a loud cheer, for being so brilliant and life-enhancing, but, this being England and not Canada, a faint grin had to suffice.

The dog was no help here. But he did make friends with actor Denis Quilley's flat-coated retrievers and the golden retrievers belonging to Labour peer Lord Gavron. He is well-acquainted with the bandanna-wearing Vinny (as in Jones), who walks at the heels of His Honour Judge Barrington Black. Beezle gets recognized by Maureen Lipman – so easy to *spot*, she says – and he reunited me with an actor friend from Oxford University days, Diana Quick, via a blue-grey lurcher almost as pretty as his owner. Diana swore she walked on the Heath every day and would wait for me by the café on the morrow. That was three years ago. I'd given up all hope when a few days ago I bumped into my magazine-editor friend Nigel Horne. He and his Lakelands collie Holly (who, unusually, does a handstand on her front paws when she pees) had just been chatting to Diana and her lurcher, he boasted. So I will give the café another try.

Writers are more incognito than performers. But if you are alert, they are as plentiful on the Heath as lesser spotted woodpeckers. David Cornwell, alias John Le Carré, used to walk a whippet when he lived in Hampstead. Playwright David Hare recently introduced me to his new puppy, Bianca. Deborah Moggach, who wrote *Tulip Fever* and *Close Relations*, is a devotee of the ladies' bathing pond. Julian Barnes, not just the author of *Flaubert's Parrot* but also the translator of a book of German dog cartoons called *Kriegels Kleine Hunde-Kunde*, may be seen from time to time striding across Parliament Hill wrapped in a funereal Charles Addams raincoat.

Margaret Forster (biographer of Daphne du Maurier) and her husband Hunter Davies (biographer of the Beatles) are keen Heathites. They even have a bench inscribed to each other to mark their silver wedding. They sometimes used to take a neighbour's springer spaniel along on walks, before he died. He was called Charlie Brown (odd, to name a spaniel not after a cartoon beagle, but after the cartoon beagle's cartoon owner). Philip Norman, another biographer of the Beatles, as well as the Rolling Stones, is a regular jogger, whose martyred look as he puffs past reminds me of all the reasons I gave up jogging myself some years ago. The *Telegraph*'s sardonic political cartoonist, Nick Garland, cycles on the Heath, wearing a sort of plastic waffle on his head. He is happy to stop and discuss the great topics of the day, which is nice for me because it reminds me of editorial conferences on the paper, when I was its deputy editor. Representing the opposite end of the media spectrum, *Guardian* guru Hugo Young walks one of those wrinkly Japanese dogs that look like bonsai hippos, and New Labour's sultan of spin, Alastair Campbell, practises sweatily for the London Marathon.

So you see, walking a dog can be a rewarding cultural experience – and not just for the dog-owner. Once, when we happened upon a scene of *Notting Hill* being shot at Kenwood House, Beezle made a sly dash for the catering trolley and wolfed a plate of ham rolls, which were the intended breakfast of Julia Roberts and Hugh Grant.

On bank holidays and summer weekends, the Heath and Kenwood are crowded with people who aren't dog-walkers at all, and don't have the excuse of being famous either. We regulars feel we are being trespassed upon and simmer with resentment. Our private wilderness becomes a public park. It is suddenly overrun with picnickers, cyclists, orienteers, charity walkers, kite-flyers, and anglers, who erect absurd little tents in which they make tea and smoke and tell you to eff off if your dog so much as sniffs at their pails of squirming maggots. This is when bossy, khaki-clad English Heritage women appear from nowhere and order you to put your dog on the lead, 'because of complaints we have received', while gay men in thongs are allowed to oil themselves and flaunt among the haycocks without so much as a raised eyebrow.

This is also when one must watch out for those pub dogs I mentioned earlier, as well as tattooed drug-dealers being hauled along by Rottweilers or Staffordshire bull-terriers with spiked collars and straining eyes. Actually, I'm a fan of Staffordshires: Beezle's first puppy friend was a tough but enchanting little Staff called Bruno, with the build of a miniature fighting bull. My wife grew up with one. I like their bounciness and big smiley heads. There is one that makes a habit of trying to pull down fully-grown oak trees with his teeth; he leaps at a lower branch, then hangs there growling through clamped jaws, jerking furiously above the ground like a small pig being lynched, until ordered to let go.

The trouble with Staffordshires in the hands of the wrong owners, I guess, is that if they do go in for biting, their faces are the wrong shape to wear a muzzle. So none of them does, which makes it hard to spot the potential snappers.

One of the many dogs in the cartoonist and writer James Thurber's life was Muggs, 'the dog that bit people'. A big, burly, choleric Airedale, 'he always acted as if he thought he wasn't one of the family', although he didn't bite the family as often as he bit strangers. Instead of muzzling the brute, young Thurber's soft-hearted mother would maintain that it wasn't the dog's fault but that of the people who were bitten.

'When he starts for them, they scream,' she explained, 'and that excites him.'

Her solution was to send a box of candy every Christmas to the people Muggs bit. The list finally contained forty or more names. When Muggs died, Thurber's mother wanted a marble headstone on his grave with some such inscription as 'Flights of angels sing thee to thy rest', but he had to make do with a bit of board on which Thurber wrote with an indelible pencil 'Cave Canem'.

'Mother', he said, 'was quite pleased with the simple dignity of the old Latin epitaph.'

Matters of Breeding

Since Christmas we have had day after day of sparkling cold and dazzling sunshine. The sun is so low on the horizon that you have to wear shades or a peaked cap to look any higher than your own feet. It is the kind of weather that starts the woodpeckers drumming to each other through the tangle of whitened treetops. The dogs race around aimlessly, kicking up little clouds of powdered frost.

For once the 'Danger: Thin Ice' signs, which droop forlornly over the ponds throughout the summer, have a purpose. The ducks ignore them and march about unconcernedly, where only a few days ago they were dabbling and diving. A swan, too heavy to do the same, pushes his chest gingerly through the floes like a Russian ice-breaker, making crackling sounds as he forges forwards.

There is no more private a public place in London than Kenwood on early mornings like these, or after a heavy snowfall. The Kenwood estate is embraced by Hampstead Heath but is not strictly part of it. Its 112 acres have a magically secluded air, the cold deepening the silence, the ancient trees forming a frozen palisade against the outside world.

You feel like an intruder into what was once that most jealously guarded of properties, the private parkland of a gentleman. The park encircles the graceful, creamy-white mansion built by Robert Adam in the 1760s, which is Kenwood House itself. Even on the night of a Kenwood summer concert, when the Pasture Ground is thronged with thousands of picnickers lolling under their lanterns, one has the sense that people feel rather smug about being there, as though they had gate-crashed Glyndebourne.

For nearly two centuries the gentleman whose parkland this was would have been one of the Earls of Mansfield. They owned Kenwood from 1755 to 1925, although in 1910 the sixth earl let it to a Russian grand duke, who installed mastiffs and gigantic Circassian guards in vulgar uniforms to protect himself, a bit like those shipping tycoons in Bishops Avenue across the way, whose modern mansions bristle with floodlights and CCTV.

Since 1928, when the house and estate became the property of the nation, we gate-crash Kenwood by right. But the sense of intrusiveness is nonetheless real, and delightful. Approach the grounds by one of the gates that lead from the Heath and you instantly notice the change. Historically, the Heath was mostly unkempt manorial grazing ground. Kenwood, by contrast, was in private hands for nearly four hundred years. As you pass from the one to the other, there is a marked difference, a sense of unobtrusive order: ancient forest, sweeping vistas, woodland glades, bogs, fields, copses, lakes, all harmoniously intermingled. This is nature domesticated. There are neatly hung bundles of green plastic bags for dog poo, unlike on the Heath.

The reason Londoners love Kenwood is that it is so faithfully in keeping with their idealized notion of the English countryside. In fact, the scenes that so please the eye are mostly the work of man, not nature, and one man in particular, Humphrey Repton, the fashionable, eighteenth-century landscape gardener, whose picturesque designs play a key role in Tom Stoppard's play *Arcadia*.

In 1793 Repton was commissioned by the second Earl of Mansfield to prepare a 'Red Book' for the Kenwood estate, with 'before' and 'after' watercolours showing the proposed improvements. His plans are very largely what we see today, though blurred here and there where scrub has invaded, new trees have seeded themselves, and older trees have grown up or tumbled down. Along these same winding, woodland walks successive Earls of Mansfield strolled with their guests, showing off the fashionable 'features' envisaged by Repton: the fake two-dimensional bridge, the model dairy, the *ferme ornée*, the meadows grazed by pure-bred cows and sheep.

When English Heritage took charge of Kenwood after the abolition of the Greater London Council in 1986, it saw its mission as not only to sort out the management of the estate after years of benign semi-neglect, but also to restore some of the lost features of this unique historic landscape. The last owner of the house, Edward Guinness, Earl of Iveagh, made it a condition of his bequeathing it to the nation that the estate should retain 'the atmosphere of a gentleman's park'.

In English Heritage's eyes, that meant a good deal of tree-felling and scrub-clearing, a purge of the rhododendron jungles and the uprooting of whole copses where, since the end of sheep-grazing, birch and alder had gained a hold.

The thinning got under way. Roused by the sound of chain-saws, the protesters moved in swiftly, led by an organization called Kenwood Trees. In 1994 English Heritage retrenched, reconsulted and reconsidered. Even its then chairman, the fiery Sir Jocelyn Stevens, agreed that a more balanced approach was needed. The responsibility for finding it fell to English Heritage's Director of Gardens and Landscape, Lorna McRobie.

Essentially, what Ms McRobie had to resolve was a horticultural version of the old nature/nurture debate. The heritage-in-aspic purists wanted to see Repton revived, even at the cost of chopping down whole clumps of mature, but inauthentic, trees. Whereas the let-nature-take-its-course brigade wanted the status quo preserved, down to the smallest sapling. They were reluctant to acknowledge that even the status quo could be maintained only by managing it. Yet rabbits kill little oaks. *Rhododendron ponticum* is a merciless invader. Walkers' boots leave scars. Trees die for lack of light or water. More than a hundred fell in the Great Storm of 1987. What then?

I interviewed Lorna McRobie for the *Evening Standard*. Like most frequent visitors to Kenwood, I leaned more towards conserving the present than restoring the past. I was against the ethnic cleansing of every tree that had had the temerity to grow where Repton did not intend it. On the other hand, walking the footpaths with Lorna, it was easy to share her enthusiasm for recovering some of the lost elements of the Mansfield parklands: the clearer views, the more gradual shading of woods into grassland, the vanished flower garden, the dairy and the stableyard as features in the grand ensemble.

But Lorna was a realist. A wiry woman who puffed away at Old Holborn roll-ups, she had her flatties firmly on the ground. She acknowledged not just the quantity but the quality of earlier protesters: this was Hampstead, after all. She accepted some of their arguments, such as the usefulness of the new 'wild' copses in breaking up open ground to make it seem less populated. Besides, she pointed out, a third of the estate now consisted of Sites of Special Scientific Interest, where Repton's writ no longer ran.

At the same time, she insisted that the estate had to be kept under control and that its historic structure should be preserved where possible. I was inclined to agree. During my dog-walking years I had watched a favourite view disappear almost utterly from sight. Mother Nature is a scatty parent. Left entirely to herself, opportunism would thrive and the 'natural' landscape so many people love would soon be smothered.

We gazed up at a towering, centuries-old beech tree, which my family particularly loved. My brothers and I had met and talked and taken a photograph at its foot after our father died, looking across the meadows at the unchanging view of Kenwood House. Well, it would have to come down one day, Lorna said briskly, before it toppled of its own accord, bringing other trees down with it. It might even kill someone. The great smooth trunk was cracked and riddled with fungus.

That was four years ago. Other fine old trees have met their ends in winter gales since then. Most have been left to lie where they fell, which pleases the wilderness bunch. I like the way the moss and toadstools take hold and the rot slowly

spreads. Sometimes you can even see a resurrection taking place, as an upper branch re-roots itself and buds of new foliage begin to appear. As for the giant beech, it was spared the axe. But only a short while ago, alas, it crashed to earth, the victim of old age and a high wind. One of my brothers and I went to mourn. It was not such a desolate sight, after all: more like a once mighty monarch, lying in state.

The dog's indifference to an ancient beech tree is hardly surprising. By contrast, there are humans who have spent years of their lives trying to trace the history of ancient dog-breeds. That of the Dalmatian is not straightforward. For a start, the one thing on which all the experts seem to agree is that the Dalmatian has nothing to do with Dalmatia, that rocky bit of the Adriatic coastline, which is now in the hands of the Croats and includes the medieval city of Dubrovnik. The first recorded Dalmatians in Dalmatia did not appear until 1926 and they, ahem, were imported.

So where did Pongo and his kind spring from? You can surf the multitude of websites in Europe and North

America devoted to the breed (they take some time to download because of all the spotty graphics and happy puppy snaps) and still not find a consensus. Drawings of blotchy dogs in Egyptian tombs and Greek caves go back thousands of years BC. India also vies for the honour of being the cradle of the carriage dog, though that was quite a while before even the wheel, let alone the carriage, was invented. At any rate, it seems that proto-Dalmatians of some description attached themselves to gypsies during the Middle Ages and thus worked their way up into central and northern Europe, developing a particular affinity for the gypsies' horses in the course of these travels. It was the dogs' close association with the Romanies, says the British Dalmatian Club mysteriously, 'that may account for their uncanny powers of communication'.

(I have tried to discover from Beezle – by means of telepathy and so on – what exactly these powers of communication might be. But apart from signalling powerfully by means of gaze, paw and head-butting that he could murder a Gravybone, he has remained silent on the matter.)

At some point during the eighteenth century, the British carriage-owning classes, ever the pioneers in dog-breeding matters, decided that Dalmatians would make elegant escorts for their equipages. They were bred to trot under the axles tirelessly for up to 40 miles a day, to deter highwaymen and hitch-hikers and generally make themselves useful on long journeys. When the carriage drew up at an inn for the evening, the Dalmatians' job was to guard the luggage and babysit the horses while the coachman and his passengers enjoyed their dinner and a night's untroubled sleep.

They were so good at this that when horse-drawn fire engines came along in the 1800s it was only natural that Dalmatians should be part of the team. Their task was not only to lead the horses to the conflagration and guard the firefighting equipment while the firemen were tackling the blaze but even, it is said, to act as rescue dogs.

I find all this hard to believe, given Beezle's hysterical reaction to any horse he has ever met and his almost suicidal love of a log fire, to the point where his nose sizzles and his whiskers singe without his moving a muscle. Nevertheless, the fashion crossed the Atlantic. Soon every firehouse in the United States had its resident Dalmatian. Two centuries on, many still do, even though the horses have gone. Over here, by contrast, British firefighters have long since neglected the PR value of having a spotted mascot riding alongside them into action. (Think what a difference that might have made to their cause in the recent strike action.)

So what of Dalmatians today? They first entered the show ring in 1860, and are still classified in the UK as 'utility' dogs. This is laughable. Let's face it, other than being handsome, companionable and supremely good-natured, they have no utility whatsoever, carriages and horse-drawn fire tenders being thin on the ground these days. My first Dalmatian once frightened off a burglar while we were asleep upstairs, before the intruder could steal the silver spoons. But Beezle, frankly, has never done a thing to earn his keep.

Nevertheless, here is a selection of what the doting web-sites say:

- Dalmatians are congenial, with a great deal of strength and stamina. They are outgoing and friendly with a courteous, gentlemanly demeanour but are also very determined. They are fast, strong and intelligent with a great deal of endurance.
- Dalmatians are people-like and people-oriented. They do best when given the opportunity to spend lots of time with and around their families. Dalmatians are rather sensitive, too – they can sulk when scolded.
- Are Dalmatians stupid? Definitely not. On the contrary, they are extremely intelligent and creative … They are often headstrong … Males, in particular, may have an independent streak.

Ho hum. Headstrong and independent, I buy. Congenial, outgoing, people-oriented? Certainly. And does Beezle sulk? Oh yes. He has perfected a kind of indignant glare, which builds up thunderously if he sees one dressing to go out in the evening or packing a suitcase, and can last a whole day if one has left him on his own too long. But gentlemanly, intelligent and *creative*?

Beezle's idea of gentlemanliness is to welcome any female visitor he likes by nuzzling her crotch, then snaking his way between her legs and emerging at the rear with her skirts over his head like a burka. I sometimes worry people will think I've trained him to do this. My elderly mother and mother-in-law enter the house on their guard, knowing they must sit down sharply or grab the banister before they're felled.

Men friends he greets in a quite different fashion, by barking loudly and prancing up and down on his front legs like a rocking horse. Come to think of it, welcoming people is what he does best, and since that is a useful social skill, it might even justify his being called a utility dog after all.

As for intelligence, it's hard to tell. Humans tend to equate canine braininess with obedience and teachability, which is why Alsatians and collies are usually thought to be top of the class. But where does instinct leave off and intelligence begin? A dog who refuses to jump through a flaming hoop is arguably brighter than the one who leaps into danger and gets his tail singed just because he's adept at doing what he's told. I am all in favour of Jilly Cooper's campaign for an Animals in War monument in Park Lane. But who's to say whether those splendid dogs who acted as messengers and ammunition-carriers in the First World War were being clever and brave or just blindly obeying orders – like most of the poor young men fighting alongside them in the trenches?

I said something earlier about how my dog has worked out that the most efficient way to target a squirrel on the ground is to head directly for the nearest tree. That seems to me extremely cunning. It can't be instinct or he'd have used the same trick when he was younger. Besides, his Dalmatian genes are unlikely to have contained much useful stuff about squirrel-chasing. I imagine the very last thing carriage dogs were permitted to do was abandon their post under the axle to race off after passing vermin.

Some people maintain that stories and films about lost dogs finding their way back to their human loved ones across miles of wilderness are proof of uncanny animal brain-power. Well, maybe dogs have some sort of homing instinct, like pigeons, or an inborn version of a cruise missile's photographic memory, but I suspect the explanation is often simpler.

My former Dalmatian had a *Lassie Come-Home/Incredible Journey* experience when he escaped from a dog-minder's in South Kensington one day and found his way back to my Notting Hill flat via the Albert Hall and Kensington Gardens. According to one reported sighting received by the police, Gus even used a pedestrian crossing to traverse the Bayswater Road.

Beezle also ran away from a temporary dog-walker, not once but twice. They were deliberate acts of protest, I think, after the tip of his tail was caught in the car door, causing a horrid injury, which took months to heal and still bleeds to this day if wagged too vigorously. On the first occasion, Beezle was found at Wood Green Tube station, where I went to collect him from a saintly passer-by, who'd clung to his collar for over forty minutes as I drove to the rescue through rush-hour traffic. On the second, he disappeared for hours one dark February evening, having last been seen miles away scampering up Turnpike Lane in the direction of Cambridge. I scoured North London in the car until long after night fell, returned home in despair, and was astonished to find him waiting for me inside the front door, bouncing up and down like a space-hopper. Our next-door neighbour had discovered him standing forlornly on the doorstep, and let him in with the spare key she kept for us.

Intelligence? Homing instinct? I think more a case of dogs' remarkable olfactory powers, allied to their habit of sniffing and peeing wherever they set foot. My belief is that Gus and Beezle simply smelled their way home, retracing their steps by means of recollected pongs and the trail of their own tenacious urine molecules. This might seem an extraordinary feat to us, but no more extraordinary than our ability to follow road signs would seem to them. John Masefield in his 1919 poem 'Reynard the Fox' praised the inhuman skill of the hounds: 'Their noses exquisitely wise / Their minds being memories of smells.'

In *The Hidden Life of Dogs*, Elizabeth Marshall Thomas watched how her pet huskies would greet one of their number on its return from a wander:

> The others would quietly surround him and investigate him for scent – the scents of his own body, which would show his state of mind and probably a great deal more as well, and the scents of the places he had been, which he carried on his fur. They'd smell his lips and his mantle, his

penis, his legs and his feet. Seldom, if ever, would they investigate his anus or anal glands, evidently because the information therefrom has to do with a dog's persona but not with his travels.

Ms Thomas knows a lot more about dogs' bottoms than most of us do.

It might seem fanciful to think dogs can interpret scents much as we might read a travel journal, but remember G.K. Chesterton's dog, Quoodle, pitying us humans for having so little sense of smell:

> They haven't got no noses,
> The fallen sons of Eve;
> Even the smell of roses
> Is not what they supposes;
> But more than mind discloses
> And more than men believe …
>
> … They haven't got no noses
> They haven't got no noses
> And goodness only knowses
> The noselessness of Man!

So, as a noseless man, I wonder whether a dog's back-tracking abilities are really so astounding after all. And no, I don't think Dalmatians are 'creative'. Nor is any other breed of dog I've ever met. Dogs are world-class attention-seekers. They know how to create a mess or a furore or the right atmosphere for a game. But so do infant humans. Digging up window boxes and scattering the earth on a cream sofa (Gus), seizing logs from the woodpile beside the hearth and shredding them on the Indian carpet (Beezle) or deliberate projectile vomiting all over her cot (baby daughter Lucy) were not creative acts at all. They were destructive and malicious, though undeniably eloquent.

According to an internet site called www.k9web.com Dalmatians can be very vocal. 'They coo and grunt and can give you a whistling yawn when attempting to avoid a scolding.' Beezle has never been heard to coo, but he yelps excitedly when approaching the Heath or seeing a cow in a field. He barks a greeting at old ladies who look like my mother or mother-in-law as we whizz by in the car. He has a remarkable repertoire of growls, ranging from the quizzical ('Don't you understand? This is *my* basket') to the aggressive ('It may be your bed, but what I say is *let sleeping dogs lie!*'). And he yawns most tellingly, with a sort of groaning, gulping sound, plus elements of swannee whistle. Sometimes this is to indicate boredom but usually extreme satisfaction, accompanied by a stretch and a supple arching of the spine. He also puffs out his cheeks like a blowfish to show impatience.

Dalmatians are famous for smiling. Not mine, which is a relief. I have seen Dalmatians that smile and it is unnerving; not so much a Cheshire cat grin as an ingratiating rictus. This may be because dogs have big teeth and no lips. At any rate k9web.com accurately describes the phenomenon as a 'smarl' – 'a combination of a smile and a snarl that can be disarming to one unfamiliar with the ways of a Dal!'

That is probably enough about 'the ways of a Dal'. But I should just mention, in case any would-be owners are reading this, that Dalmatians also shed a continuous, invisible storm of tiny white hairs. These hairs go everywhere. I toyed with the idea of calling this book *Snow Falling on Sofas*. I have looked at these hairs under a microscope and they have minute hooks on them. They attach themselves like grappling irons to every passing object. This is why Dalmatians look as wonderfully clean as they always do and why there tends to be a slightly fuzzy aura about the appearance of their human friends. Sensible owners should learn to keep their dogs off the furniture and eschew dark clothing. Alas, we have done neither. I bet the inventor of Velcro had a Dalmatian.

Dogs of Renown

None of the above seems to have deterred otherwise intelligent people from owning Dalmatians. Picasso had one. George Washington and Benjamin Franklin were both fans. So was another famous American, the playwright Eugene O'Neill, author of *Long Day's Journey Into Night*.

In 1940 O'Neill's wife Carlotta was very upset by the death of the family's beloved Dalmatian. To comfort her, he wrote *The Last Will and Testament of Silverdene Emblem O'Neill*, familiarly known as Blemie. O'Neill imagines the dying Blemie in philosophical vein:

> It is time I said goodbye, before I become too sick
> a burden on myself and on those who love me.
> It will be sorrow to leave them, but not a sorrow
> to die. Dogs do not fear death as men do. What
> may come after death, who knows? I would like to
> believe with those of my fellow Dalmatians who
> are devout Mohammedans, that there is a Paradise
> where one is always young and full-bladdered;

where all the day one dillies and dallies with an
amorous multitude of houris, beautifully spotted;
where jack rabbits that run fast but not too fast
(like the houris) are as the sands of the desert;
where each blissful hour is mealtime; where in
long evenings there are a million fireplaces with
logs forever burning, and one curls oneself up
and blinks into the flames and nods and dreams,
remembering the brave old days on earth, and
the love of one's Master and Mistress.

This passage shows how even the searing playwright of *The Iceman Cometh* could get a bit gooey when writing about dogs. It is a common problem, this soppification of the relationship between writer and faithful hound. Even sensible authors, who would never dare eulogize their own children in this adoring way, succumb.

John Galsworthy wrote a long, touching and deeply sentimental essay about an old black gun-dog. It was really about man's love affair with dogs in general, a subject hard to approach without sounding mawkish. The essence of this companionship, he said, does not depend on the dog's good points or particular usefulness,

but on some strange and subtle mingling of mute
spirits. For it is by muteness that a dog becomes
for one so utterly beyond value; with him one is at
peace, where words play no torturing tricks. When
he just sits, loving, and knows that he is being loved,
those are the moments that I think are precious to
a dog; when, with his adoring soul coming through
his eyes, he feels that you are really thinking of him.

This is pretty sick-making – unless you happen to be a dog-
owner yourself and have struggled to explain this sense of
dumb companionship, which is at once so deeply satisfying
and yet faintly shaming, not to say yucky. What makes it
shaming is the suspicion that there is an element of *worship*
involved, which goes beyond mere gratitude for board and
lodging. What makes it yucky is that the worship is sometimes mutual.

Maurice Maeterlinck, the Belgian winner of the Nobel
Prize for literature of 1911, is candid on this delicate subject.
Among all the world's creatures, including man, the dog is
uniquely privileged, he thinks:

He is the only living being that has found and
recognizes an indubitable, tangible, unexceptionable
and definite god. He knows what to devote the best

part of himself to. He knows who it is, above himself, that he gives himself to.

Kipling makes the same point in 'Thy Servant', supposedly spoken by a loyal old dog approaching his death-bed:

> Master, pity Thy Servant! He is deaf and three
> parts blind,
> He cannot catch Thy Commandments. He cannot
> read Thy Mind.
> Oh, leave him not in his loneliness; nor make him
> that kitten's scorn.
> He has had no other God than Thee since the year
> that he was born!

There may be something in this, though I suspect (a) it tells us more about the human yearning to receive unconditional love than a dog's desire to give it, and (b) it makes no mention of the biscuit factor. But you can see that when we come to talking about the relationship between dog and man, or woman, it concerns something a good deal more complicated than mere companionship.

One of the world's most famous literary dogs was Elizabeth Barrett Browning's spaniel Flush. Penning an encomium to the creature for being such a devoted presence in her sickroom, the knotty poet of 'How do I love thee? Let me count the ways' gives herself over to mooning about 'sleek curls' and 'silken ears':

> Blessings on thee, dog of mine,
> Pretty collars make thee fine,
> Sugared milk make fat thee!
> Pleasures wag on in thy tail,
> Hands of gentle motion fail
> Nevermore, to pat thee!

After twenty verses of this, one holds one's nose and wishes one could help Flush live up to his name. By contrast, Robert Herrick's epitaph for his spaniel Tracie is brisk and affecting:

> Now thou art dead, no eye shall ever see
> For shape and service spaniel like to thee.
> This shall my love do, give thy sad death one
> Tear, that deserves of me a million.

Poets tend to slip into mock-heroics when mourning the passing of a favourite dog, perhaps to disguise their real sense of loss. Byron admitted that the rather grandiose lines he wrote commemorating the death of his great black and white Newfoundland, Boatswain, who had been his companion as a Cambridge undergraduate, 'would be unmeaning flattery if inscribed over Human Ashes'. So they would. The final couplet reads: 'To mark a friend's remains these stones arise; / I never knew but one – and here he lies.' Nevertheless, they are introduced by a genuinely moving epitaph:

Near this spot
Are deposited the Remains
Of one
Who Possessed Beauty
Without Vanity,
Strength without Insolence,
Courage without Ferocity,
And all the Virtues of Man
Without his Vices.

Not even many dogs could aspire to such an encomium.

Evidently, I have been doing some background reading. The Maeterlinck passage comes from a beguiling little book by the French writer Roger Grenier, *Les larmes d'Ulysse*. The title is a reference to Ulysses' faithful old hound Argus, who was the only one to recognize the home-coming hero and who thereupon died at his master's feet. The English version is elegantly translated by Alice Kaplan but has the more plodding title, *The Difficulty of Being a Dog*.

The book is very French, which is to say that a lot of its philosophical observations and sly *aperçus* are above my head. Grenier draws on Rilke, Rousseau, Voltaire, Stendhal, Proust, Baudelaire, Gide, D.H. Lawrence and Virginia Woolf, among other unexpected sages, to explore the strange symbiosis between dog and man. A typical reflection arises from the story of a Jewish prisoner of the Nazis during the war. To his captors, the prisoner and his fellow Jews no longer belonged to the human race. But on a work-party one day, they were joined by a stray dog, who plainly appreciated their company. 'For the dog,' said the Jew, 'there was no doubt we were men.' There is not much scope for doggy jokes in this kind of thing.

Noting that Rilke reproaches dogs for not living as long as we do, Grenier observes gloomily:

> Each day, by the brevity of its life, our pet tells us,
> I shall soon be dead. In the deepest sense, these
> familiar creatures are part of the hurt of living.
> Because dogs inflict the suffering of loss upon us,
> the French sometimes call them 'beasts of sorrow',
> *bêtes de chagrin.*

Napoleon himself was not immune to this kind of despondency. In the *Memorial of Saint Helena* Bonaparte remembers how he was once walking across a battlefield from which the corpses had not yet been removed when he saw a dog at its dead master's side, howling and licking his face. He wrote:

> No incident, on any of my battlefields, ever
> produced so deep an impression on me. I had,
> without emotion, ordered battles that were to
> decide the fate of the army; I had beheld, with
> a dry eye, the execution of these operations, by
> which numbers of my countrymen were sacrificed;
> and here I was upset, my feelings roused, by the
> mournful howling of a dog.

When Bonaparte married Josephine, Grenier notes drily, 'she refused to kick a pug named Fortuné out of her bed. Fortuné was used to sleeping with her, so the general was forced to share the Creole beauty's bed with her dog.' Perhaps what Napoleon really said, in a tone of exasperation, was, 'Not tonight, Fortuné.'

I don't much care for pugs myself, but here is Stevie Smith's funny and touching poem, 'O Pug!', about a friend's dog who belonged to this maybe not so *fortuné* breed:

O Pug, some people do not like you,
But I like you,
Some people say you do not breathe, you snore,
I don't mind,
One person says he is always conscious of your
  behind,
Is that your fault?

Your own people love you,
All the people in the family that owns you
Love you: Good pug, they cry, Happy pug,
Pug-come-for-a-walk.

You are an old dog now
And in all your life
You have never had cause for a moment's anxiety,
Yet,
In those great eyes of yours,
Those liquid and protuberant orbs,
Lies the shadow of immense insecurity. There
Panic walks.

Yes, yes, I know,
When your mistress is with you,
When your master
Takes you upon his lap,

Just then, for a moment,
Almost you are not frightened.

But at heart you are frightened, you always
   have been.

O Pug, obstinate old nervous breakdown,
In the midst of *so* much love,
And such comfort,
Still to feel unsafe and be afraid,

   How one's heart goes out to you!

Compared with Stevie Smith's compassion, Grenier's general drift seems to be: dog as intruder on the human condition, dog as *memento mori*. British readers will feel more comfortable when he quotes the life-affirming author of *Elizabeth and Her German Garden* and *Enchanted April*.

Elizabeth von Arnim, the cousin of Katherine Mansfield, called her wonderfully original autobiography, first published in 1936, *All the Dogs of My Life*. It opens with the unforgettable line: 'I would like, to begin with, to say that though parents, husbands, children, lovers, and friends are all very well, they are not dogs.' How true.

This was her advice, recollecting a spell of lonely widowhood:

I recommend those persons of either sex, but chiefly, it would seem, of mine, whose courage is inclined to fail them if they are long alone, who are rather frightened in the evenings if there is nobody to speak to, who don't like putting out their own lights and climbing silently to a solitary bedroom, who are full of affection and have nothing to fasten it on to, who long to be loved and, for whatever reason, aren't – I would recommend all such to go, say, to Harrods, and buy a dog … in eager rows, they will find a choice of friends, only waiting to be given a chance of cheering and protecting. Asking nothing in return, either, and, whatever happens, never going to complain, never going to be cross, never going to judge, and against whom no sin committed will be too great for immediate and joyful forgiveness. Saints, in fact. Cheerful saints, too, which is, I think, important. And numerous, no doubt, as our human saints are, and worthy to be exalted, it would be difficult to find among them a more complete saint than a good dog.

Feeling as she did, no wonder Elizabeth von Arnim measured out her life in dogs. She had fourteen of them.

Fourteen dogs in sequence over a lifetime is one thing. Encountering such a number all at the same moment, bursting out of a wood towards you, can cause a moment's panic. Perhaps the sight of so many teeth and jowls stirs some primitive fear of the wolf pack. But the moment passes when you notice that these dogs are to *Canis lupus* what a tabby cat is to a tiger. They are mostly small and hairy or soft and fluffy, and the brightness in their eyes is not that of ravening killers but of urchins on a spree.

Marching along in their midst is a striking figure in stout boots and heavy eye-liner. This is Suzy Crabtree, the Heath's most famous dog-walker. She has long green fingernails, which are clamped around a great bundle of snaky leads so that it looks as if she's carrying the severed head of a Gorgon. She has a commanding voice, which, as she puts it, 'would carry in a Force Ten gale across a hockey pitch'. This being unreliable March, she wears a broad-brimmed hat. In the summer she favours leggings and totes a water-pistol stuck into a low-slung leather belt. Her own dog, Baggins, a mixture of poodle and Tibetan terrier, echoes the cowboy theme by wearing a red bandanna tied loosely round his neck. Fourteen charges is, I think, the most I've seen her with, though ten or a dozen is quite usual.

'They fancy themselves as a gang of adventure-hungry desperados,' Suzy says, 'but battling with hazards no greater than squirrels and rabbits.'

There are other dog-walkers who roam the Heath with four or five dogs at their heels, though none is as colourful as Ms Crabtree, who has written in *The Times*, appeared on Radio 4 and been a subject of the *Sunday Times*'s 'A Life In The Day Of' feature.

Sometimes one dog-walker will run into another. You would have thought that at this point primal wolfish behaviour would assert itself and the two packs would bridle and snarl at each other. Not a bit of it. While their human minders chat, the twenty or so dogs around them will mingle and play as happily as puppies on a lawn. There is an interesting phenomenon at work here. While single dogs out with their owners tend to be individualistic and assertive, as members of a dog-walker's pack they seem to become as biddable as infants, casting aside their usual sense of dignity without a qualm. Suzy, who was a drama teacher before she became an alpha dog-walker, says dogs are 'just like four-year-old children, and the psychology for both is the same'. She seldom uses either lead or water-pistol, though she did once have to swim a river fully-dressed to retrieve a straying basset hound. At the end of the walk she simply musters the troops.

'Megan, Zara, Izzy, Lolly, Buffy, Bobby, Alfie, Milo, Billy, and my old Bag. Come, stay, sit!' she barks. 'There they are. All of them. It's a little miracle that happens every day.'

Performing dogs

If a group of supervised dogs is like a class of small children with their teacher, the one-to-one relationship between a dog and its owner is closer to that of teenager and parent: affectionate when there is some reward to be had, such as a £20 note or a ticket to Australia, otherwise forever testing the boundaries of independence. That is a more comforting analogy than you might think, the reassuring bit for dog-owners being that dogs mature a good deal faster than adolescents and don't take gap-years.

The American photographer Elliott Erwitt does not altogether agree with this comparison. In his marvellous book of dog pictures, *Dogdogs*, he writes about his subjects' childlike innocence and lack of guile, but adds that they are not exactly like children:

> They are more nonchalant. They don't necessarily want you to notice that they are around, because they know that they belong.
>
> Dogs don't have to say 'Look at me!' the way

children often do. However, they are more unfocused than children. For one thing they are forced to lead a life that is really schizoid. Every day they must live on two planes at once, juggling the dog world with the human world. And they're always on call. Their owners demand instant affection every day, any time of day. A dog can never say that he has a headache or other things to do.

I don't know about that last bit. Dogs often take command. In a jolly essay in Erwitt's book, P.G. Wodehouse remembers an Aberdeen terrier called Angus, the original of Stiffy Byng's Bartholomew in *The Code of the Woosters*. Angus was a rigid Calvinist, Wodehouse writes:

> [He] had a way of standing in front of me and looking at me like a Scottish preacher about to rebuke the sins of his congregation. Sundays with him were particularly trying. There is almost nothing you can do on a Sunday which does not arouse the disapproval of an Aberdeen terrier.

After Angus was given away to someone less prone to whistle on the Sabbath, Wodehouse and his wife 'fell under the spell of Pekes'. They had a good many of these, including

Bimmy, Boo, Loopy, Mrs Miffen, Squeaky and Miss Winks. The great man wrote:

> Many people, I know, disparage Pekes, but take it from me, they are all right. If they have a fault, it is a tendency to think too much of themselves. One can readily understand it, of course. For centuries they belonged only to Emperors. If you were not an Emperor and were found with a Peke on your premises, you got the Death of a Thousand Cuts … But none of our Pekes pulled rank on us. They could not have been more democratic and affable.

Wodehouse raised a question that has troubled many a dog-owner: do dogs have a sense of humour?

> My own opinion [he says] is that some have and some don't. Dachshunds have, but not St Bernards and Great Danes. It would seem that a dog has to be small to be fond of a joke. You never find an Irish wolfhound trying to be a stand-up comic.

Alas, I think he is avoiding the simple truth, which is that there are dogs that *look* clownish and those that don't. There is no evidence at all of dogs getting a kick out of making humans laugh, never mind amusing each other. Photographer William Wegman's trench-coated Weimaraners are marvellously lugubrious, but they show no sign of sharing the joke.

There was a Weimaraner we used to encounter regularly on our walks who certainly made people grin, but I don't believe his intentions were comical. His long-suffering mistress might have wished they were. He was simply the naughtiest dog on the Heath. His name was Henry. He was very big and had a crazed look in his pale-blue eyes. He once swam out to a small island in one of the ponds and refused to return. He spent the whole day there looking challengingly across the water, playing Robinson Crusoe while his mistress called to him pathetically from the shore. Only when night fell and supper beckoned did he consent to swim back to the mainland.

A favourite gambit of Henry's was to scavenge for titbits in the square, waist-high, wooden rubbish bins. He would leap in lightly, then proceed to toss out everything he found inside that wasn't edible. All the onlooker would see was what looked like a volcano of litter erupting from the bin, with Coke cans and carrier bags shooting into the sky. In the midst of this explosive display could be discerned the tip of a thick grey tail, wagging joyfully. Everyone knew to whom it belonged.

Dalmatians are frequently used in commercials, because of all the amusing things that can be done with their spots. Beezle has posed alongside models in dotty dresses and featured in a mystifying ad for a bar-coding system on French medical packaging.

Like all family dogs, he has also been dressed up from time to time in bonnets, shawls, wellington boots, sunglasses, etc. Last year he starred in our Christmas card, wearing a scarlet bobble hat. But let's face it, apart from appreciating the connection between camera and biscuit, he treats these performances with indifference and no trace of either smile or smarl.

Even show dogs are not always that keen to strut their stuff. James Thurber had a standard French poodle called Medve (Hungarian for 'bear'). She was often in the ring, but hated public appearances. According to Thurber:

> Medve's profound dislike of show business caused her to develop a kind of Freudian car-sickness, because riding in a car had so often meant a trip to the dog show … She was made to wear a red rubber bib, tied around her neck, and a newspaper was always placed on the floor of the car. She threw

up on it like a lady, leaning far down, looking as
apologetic as she looked sick.

This strikes a chord. One of the most embarrassing things
that can happen to a dog-owner is to have one's dog throw
up in someone else's car. It happened to friends of ours.
They had a Highland terrier called Flora, whom they had
bought in the belief that a dog would enhance their lives.
She made so many messes on the carpets, she was ironically known as The Life-Enhancer. They were being given
a lift through Islington when The Life-Enhancer suddenly
gave a yip and threw up all over the back seat. As it happened, it was my car. The very particular smell lingered for
years. How a small dog could have found and consumed a
side of salt cod and a whole ripe Camembert in our back
garden we shall never know.

Thurber's *New Yorker* colleague E.B. White, author of
Charlotte's Web, had a dog who also gave trouble in cars. He
was a dachshund, or 'dash-hound', called Fred:

He was red and low-posted and long-bodied like
a dachshund, and when you glanced casually at
him he certainly gave the quick impression of
being a dachshund. But if you went at him with

a tape-measure, and forced him on to scales,
the dachshund theory collapsed.

In any event, Fred was not a very loving dog, White recalls:

> The only time he was ever discovered in an attitude
> that suggested affection was when I was in the
> driver's seat of the car and he would lay his heavy
> head on my right knee. This, I soon perceived,
> was not affection, it was nausea. Drooling always
> followed, and the whole thing was extremely
> inconvenient, because the weight of his head
> made me press too hard on the accelerator.

I am quoting from a splendid anthology called *Old Dogs
Remembered*, edited by Bud Johns. It includes engaging pieces
by White and Thurber as well as the O'Neill Dalmatian's
last will and testament, the Galsworthy threnody and the
poetic epitaphs I mentioned earlier. On the whole,
humorists make the sharper observers of canine behaviour,
I'd say. For example E.B. White encapsulates whole chapters
of dog psychology when he describes Fred succinctly as
having the 'devotion of an opportunist'.

To Fred, the Whites' four-poster bed represented 'the
happy heights':

Once up, he settled into his pose of bird watching, propped luxuriously against a pillow, as close as he could get to the window, his great soft brown eyes alight with expectation and scientific knowledge. He seemed never to tire of his work. He watched steadily and managed to give the impression that he was a secret agent of the Department of Justice. Spotting a flicker or a starling on the wing, he would turn and make a quick report. 'I just saw an eagle go by,' he would say. 'It was carrying a baby.'

Talking of dogs talking, the strong, Disney-fuelled wish that dogs could speak must be almost universal. In sensible folk, however, the fantasy is kept in check by fear of what the dear, dumb creatures would say if suddenly blessed with human speech. At best, one might be treated to a stream of banalities about discarded chicken wings or disgusting

smells; at worst, a diatribe of criticism, as from a disgruntled employee, demanding longer walks, more varied menus and greater respect. Bang would go the whole sentimental notion of unconditional love.

But this has never put off cartoonists. They are addicted to the talking dog, whose role as both put-upon pet and domestic insider gives him a unique chance to play the ironist. 'It's always "Sit", "Stay" "Heel",' says one indignant pooch in a Peter Steiner cartoon, 'never "Think", "Innovate", "Be yourself".' In the *New Yorker*, which specializes in this area, dogs not only talk but also muse, read, write and have a lofty understanding of the human condition. In another Steiner gag, a dog sits on the hearthrug listening intelligently while a small, bespectacled man in a bow tie addresses him thus: 'I've told you why I need a dog. Now suppose you tell me what makes you think you might be that dog.' Snoopy, who does his talking in thought-bubbles rather than out loud, is not merely the equal of Charlie Brown, Lucy, Linus and the rest of the gang. In point of literacy, history, philosophy and psychology he is their effortless superior. He can even interpret the twitterings of Woodstock, whose runic, exclamation-mark language would have defeated the Enigma code-breakers.

At around five to six each evening, Beezle stares at the kitchen radio with rapt attention. As the bongs begin to strike he leaps up with an alert and eager expression. If he could speak he would say, 'I think you'll find that is Big Ben, announcing my supper-time.'

April makes me downhearted, not just because of T.S. Eliot's haunting opening lines in *The Waste Land*, but because in England it is a time of so much promise, so often betrayed by the brevity of spring and summer. Dogs' lives are sadly short, too. If you want to be gloomy about it, owning a dog is a sure prelude to mourning, hence Grenier's *bêtes de chagrin*.

'It would seem that the more you care for a dog, and the more care you take of him, the more, as it were, he dies,' wrote Elizabeth von Arnim. And this is Ogden Nash on the subject, 'For A Good Dog':

My little dog ten years ago
Was arrogant and spry,
Her backbone was a bended bow
For arrows in her eye.
Her step was proud, her bark was loud,
Her nose was in the sky,
But she was ten years younger then,
And so, by God, was I.

Small birds on stilts along the beach
Rose up with piping cry,
And as they flashed beyond her reach
I thought to see her fly.
If natural law refused her wings,
That law she would defy,
For she could do unheard-of-things,
And so, at times, could I.

Ten years ago she split the air
To seize what she could spy;
Tonight she bumps against the chair,
Betrayed by milky eye.
She seems to pant, Time up, time up!
My little dog must die,
And lie in dust with Hector's pup;
So, presently, must I.

The biographer and novelist Victoria Glendinning (who once assured her Heath-walking friends Lord Gavron and his wife Kate that dogs were not a child-substitute; speaking as both mother and dog-owner she maintained it was the other way round) still finds herself moved by the obituary of her dog Sophy, which she wrote for the diary column of a weekly magazine:

Sophy Dog died peacefully at Coolnaclehy on
25 August. She was 17 years old, a handsome bitch
of medium size, tricoloured, with a crooked white
stripe down her long, elegant nose. Her mother
was partly collie, her father was partly Alsatian,
and there were Jack Russells among her ancestry.
All her life she divided her time between London
and Ireland, greatly preferring the latter.

Her most noticeable characteristic was her
peculiarly sharp bark. Possessed of strong territorial
instincts, she barked at all comers, and at anyone
who even passed the house, until in late life deafness
and cataract dimmed her perceptions. Many
found her excessively tiresome; but those in her
confidence will not soon forget her loyalty, her
grace, her intelligence, her powers of intuition,
and her discretion. Sharing as she so intimately
did the strange vicissitudes of her owner's life,
Sophy carries many secrets to her grave. She
never married.

That is indeed an obit which, for lapidary affection, without sentiment, matches Byron's epitaph for Boatswain.

There are more accounts of humans losing beloved dogs
than the other way around, though Freud was survived by

a chow called Lun who shunned the father of psycho-analysis as he lay dying of cancer, which greatly saddened him, and Greyfriars Bobby famously outlived his master.

In *Old Dogs Remembered* there is a poem by John Updike about the solitary death of a family's new puppy, which is heartbreaking and should certainly be kept out of the hands of young dog-owners. There is also an essay by the popular nineteenth-century American nature writer John Burroughs. When his fox terrier Nip died in 1898, Burroughs wrote in his diary: 'Of all the domestic animals none calls forth so much love, solicitude, and sorrow as the dog. He occupies the middle place between the other animals and man.'

There's something in that, whatever cat-lovers might say. But maybe it is a touch too sweeping and reverential. The English language suggests that dogs are generally held in low esteem. On the whole, canine metaphors are unflattering: cur, whelp, mongrel, son of a bitch, bitchy, dog-in-a-manger, dog-eared, dog days, going to the dogs, and so on. An ugly woman is described as a dog. Churchill called his bouts of depression the Black Dog. Although Theseus in *A Midsummer Night's Dream* is allowed to praise his Spartan-bred hounds – 'With ears that sweep away the morning dew; / Crook-knee'd, and dew-lapp'd like Thessalian bulls; / Slow in pursuit, but match'd in mouth like bells' – Shakespeare does not seem to have been much of a dog-lover, either. Shylock is indignant at being called a dog. Othello, describing how he has done the state some service, tells how he dealt with a malignant Turk: 'I took by the throat the circumcised dog / And smote him thus.' In Coriolanus's eyes the ordinary people are 'the common cry of curs whose breath I hate'. There is not much evidence here that dogs occupy 'the middle place between the other animals and man'.

People say 'it's a dog's life', implying disdain for the lowly tedium and slavishness of the canine routine (no one says 'it's a cat's life'). Yet there is some ambiguity about the phrase, it seems to me. I detect a certain jealousy for the untroubled nature of a pet dog's existence: fed, watered, walked and cared for without ever having to take a jot of responsibility for itself. Thurber's lop-eared cartoon canines seem far more at ease with the world than their diminutive

browbeaten masters and termagant mistresses. 'You ought to spend more time with your own species,' yells one of the latter spitefully, addressing a particularly inoffensive-looking hound.

This uncomplicated attitude to the world was exemplified by Thurber's own childhood pet, a bull terrier called Rex, who loved carrying things around in his mighty jaws. One day Rex dragged home a whole chest of drawers he had found on a rubbish dump, probably for no better reason than that 'it presented a nice problem in transportation'. On Hampstead Heath one often sees dogs, especially Labradors, staggering along with huge tree-branches clamped in their mouths, apparently just to please themselves.

Thurber thought humans showed 'a curious streak of envy' with regard to dogs, 'akin to what psychiatrists know as sibling jealousy. Man is troubled by what might be called the Dog Wish, a strange and involved compulsion to be as happy and carefree as a dog.'

A Dog Down Under

I have just been reminded of the danger of dipping into other people's books, which is what we journalists call 'research'. My sister-in-law in Sydney sent me a present she thought would be just up my street. It was an attractive little book printed in an elegant typeface on cream paper, and it had a very poor drawing of a dog's head on the cover. It was called *Walking Ella: A dog day dossier*. It was by a famous Australian writer called Robert Drewe. I began to read.

By page two I was laughing at the description of an uncontrollably greedy dog called Ella creating havoc at an Indian family picnic in Sydney's Centennial Park. On page three, my laughter changed to a slightly uneasy chuckle. Ella, wrote Robert Drewe,

> might look like a dog – a handsome, liver-coloured,
> spayed, German shorthaired pointer bitch – but
> she's actually a sort of anti-dog. She doesn't fetch
> or come, or even favour a particular person. While
> she probably prefers our family to strangers she'll

betray us for anyone with a bag of chips or a
ham sandwich.

I had a creeping sense not so much of *déjà vu* as *déjà écrit*.

By page eight there was no getting away from it. 'It occurs
to me,' mused the author of *The Drowner* and *The Bay of
Contented Men*,

> that it might be cathartic to write a dog-walker's
> journal: the true, unsentimental ruminations of a
> dog-walker with things on his mind more important
> than dogs. A dog-walker who, frankly, prefers
> humans. A dog-walker who decides to make the
> most of this begrudged walk to mull over writing
> ideas and dilemmas. A prickly, grumpy, even
> sometimes hung-over dog-walker.

Oh dear, oh dear. Here were two sometimes hungover middle-aged men on opposite sides of the world, both earning
their crust from writing, both dog-owners, both committed
to walking the brute on a daily basis and both with the same
idea for making something of it. Except that Mr Drewe's
book was published in 1998 while mine was not yet even
written. Except that he was a prize-winning novelist and I
was not. Oh gloom.

In the journalistic world where I have worked most of my life a newspaper will often throw out its own story or reduce it to a few paragraphs rather than be seen to have been scooped by a rival. What should I do? Give up my little book? Read no more of Robert Drewe's and proceed as if I didn't know of its existence? Or read on, make an effort to avoid even unconscious plagiarism, and confess to the coincidence?

It was no contest. *Walking Ella* was much too funny for me not to finish it. Besides, I reasoned, writing a book about dogs was hardly the most original idea in the world. And in any case, surely walking a German shorthaired pointer bitch in baking hot Sydney must be a very different experience from sloshing through the London mud with a male Dalmatian.

Well, yes and no. In terms of what Americans call 'behaviors' our dogs don't seem to be all that different, though Ella, being spayed, is emphatically into food rather than sex. She seems to be a far more heroic guzzler than Beezle, her eclectic menus including 'everything from a drunk's vomit outside the Windsor Castle to stolen Thai leftovers or a road-killed cat'. The range of wildlife in Centennial Park is also a great deal more exotic than the rabbits and squirrels Beezle is likely to flush on Hampstead Heath (though we were once startled to see an emerald-green parrot fly over our heads). Ella encounters possums, pelicans, sacred ibises and even octopus, though admittedly they are mostly dead. She either wolfs the stiffened corpses immediately or carries them about in triumph, scandalizing the park's mothers and children.

Here and there, though, our paths merge. As regards dog-walking etiquette, for example, Drewe's observations tally pretty closely with my own:

> There is a definite park protocol for saying hello.
> Before 7.30 a.m. there is greater camaraderie
> between individual dog-walking strangers. It's
> OK then, almost compulsory, to say good morning.
> (But only if he or she, like you, has a dog in tow.)
> There is a hearty feeling that both of you are in
> this early-morning activity together, and are maybe
> even a little intrepid.
>
> After 8 a.m. the friendliness dwindles to a nod.
> [Alert readers will note that the Hampstead Heath
> timetable differs somewhat in this respect.] The
> nod gets curter as the day progresses. Speaking is
> out, unless you both have the same breed of dog,
> of course, in which case you're members of the
> same club, like MG drivers, and are welcome to
> speak freely at any hour, comparing their habits,

misadventures and dire effects on your lives. The
same freedom applies when one of you is walking
a very small puppy …

Saying hello in the park after sunset is not done.
No one who isn't a same-breed owner or puppy
owner and/or a cruising homosexual says hello
at or after dusk.

Aha. So these behaviour patterns are international. This
would be my defence in a plagiarism case. But, interestingly, where I accuse Canadian dog-walkers like my brother
of ignoring these rules by being cloyingly over-friendly,
Robert Drewe makes the same point about *us*, the taciturn
Brits, if you can believe it:

Mind you, the hearty greeting of ambulant
strangers can be quite tedious and exhausting, as
anyone walking in England's Lake District, home
of the compulsory early-morning hello (and last
haunt of hikers in tweed plus-fours), can attest.

Pish tush. Didn't he realize those plus-fours-wearing hello-
sayers up on the fells were probably Germans? But aside
from this minor misapprehension, *Walking Ella* is a gem.
I commend it to dog-walkers everywhere.

Drewe raises the subject of outdoor sex among humans. Ella has a keen nose for a used condom, which she is prone to swing around in her teeth, attracting audiences of toddlers and their embarrassed parents. In this part of London, gay men tend to confine their al fresco activities to the northern bit of the Heath, on the other side of Hampstead Lane, where the detritus of discarded condoms deters most dog-walkers. So Beezle has none of Ella's savoir-faire in this regard.

He and I have only once come across *in flagrante* copulation and that was ostentatiously heterosexual. It was about 7.30 on a sunny Saturday morning. The couple made no attempt at concealment and were banging away on a grassy hillside close to a path. They were stark naked and heedless of the startled passers-by, who paused, stared incredulously at the man's bouncing buttocks, then walked on with an embarrassed grin on their lips. It was an oddly disturbing sight. While the pair's activities might have been allowable in a *Cider With Rosie*-ish setting among the haystooks, here amidst the polite decorum of the Heath it seemed like social anarchy. It was, well, uncouth.

Twenty minutes later I looked back down from the crest of Parliament Hill and they were still at it, the girl with her knees in the air and the man's bottom rising and falling with the dull regularity of a porn star's. One had to admire their stamina. One also had to admit that midnight skinny-dipping in the ladies' bathing pond thirty years ago, which was as adventurous as I had ever got on Hampstead Heath, was nowhere near as daring.

On the whole the Heath and Kenwood are not notably sexy places. They do not exude the furtive libidinous energy of the Bois de Boulogne or Central Park. Except on summer concert nights, the young are easily outnumbered by the middle-aged and elderly. All the same, the solitary early-morning walker is allowed the odd fantasy. For a couple of years there was a tall, slim, blonde girl I would occasionally see power-walking along the paths as the sun rose, earphones in place. Tied to her belt was a saluki who loped along behind her. She looked strikingly like Princess Diana, who at that time was still alive and notorious for her escapades. I never spoke to this woman, but every day I hoped to catch a glimpse of her. I saw other men stop to watch her go by, too. Today, alas, we must be content with a far less transfixing spectacle, that of a large, determined-looking man going for his morning jog. It is Diana's biographer, Andrew Morton.

AUGUST
Agony and Ecstasy

As for Beezle's sex-life, which never amounted to very much, it has lately ceased to be altogether. When a dog gets an enlarged prostate, the cure is even more drastic than it is for a man.

'I am afraid zis means castration,' said our vet's new partner, peeling off her surgical gloves with an air of solemnity. She said 'zis' because she was French, which made her diagnosis the more convincing. Had she been English, I might have suspected some sort of anti-male thing. As it was, she gave her verdict with an expression of worldly sorrow and I accepted it stoically. Beezle was unmoved, his gaze glued to the tin where the vet kept *bonbons* to reward good patients.

We asked for a reprieve so as to give him a chance of fathering a litter before he had the chop. A friend had told us of a pretty, liver-spotted Dalmatian bitch who was in search of a husband. Beezle and I went courting. Meg was at home – we could see her through the frosted glass of the front door – but her owners were not. At that moment a neighbour arrived to take Meg for a walk and told us her owners were away. Beezle and the would-be mother of his puppies, who was indeed very pretty, met on the pavement outside her house. They sniffed each other with interest while I wrote a note offering love, marriage and guarantees of champion pedigree. Alas, we never heard back. His last hope of romance was dashed. That was the beginning and end of Beezle's version of *Brief Encounter*.

For twenty-four hours after he'd had the operation he absolutely refused to look at me. To begin with, this could be put down to post-anaesthetic grogginess; on the way back from the vet's he tried to sit up in his usual co-pilot position in the car but kept toppling over with a puzzled expression on his face and crashing into the windscreen. Once this had worn off, however, it was plain he was engaged in a massive sulk and that he held me personally responsible for what had happened. I could not blame him. In place of those jaunty balls of his he now had a sad little purse, which flapped emptily when he walked. Perhaps I should have asked the vet to install a pair of prosthetic substitutes. They would have salvaged Beezle's pride and given him something to lick when lying by the fireside.

At least he didn't try to lick the operation wound. Had he done so we would have had to humiliate him further by putting him into one of those cone-shaped collars that make the wearers look like four-legged lampshades. Gus was something of a pioneer in this field back in the early 1970s. He had been badly bitten in one of his hind legs by a pair of salukis, who coursed him like a hare. My friend Bruce Fogle, celebrity vet and best-selling author, was on the case. He was concerned that Gus would gnaw the wound and pull out the stitches. So we cut the bottom out of a plastic bucket and fastened it over his head with bits of tape lashed to his collar. It was a fairly primitive arrangement, and Gus kept blundering into things because the bucket gave him tunnel vision. But it did the trick, and paved the way for the fancy transparent items we see today.

So far, Beezle's eunuch state seems to have had no adverse effects. He has not put on weight or become any less boisterous. This morning he actually made a pass at a flirtatious Rhodesian ridgeback. His bark is still a light tenor. My daughters say he is a bit less growly, but I suspect that's just more anti-male propaganda. In the meantime I have noticed that on cold days the sad little purse puckers up so that it almost looks as if its former contents were still within. This phenomenon puts a spring in Beezle's step and, for a moment, assuages my lingering guilt.

There has been another development this summer. We met Dima Yeremenko. He was standing beside Henry Moore's

Two Piece Reclining Figure No. 5 in the grounds of Kenwood House. Even at a distance and wearing a baseball hat, there was a commanding air about him.

Around the base of the sculpture lay some half a dozen other reclining figures, far more pleasing to the eye than Moore's truncated shapes. They were placidly twitching their tails and yawning, but never once did they take their eyes off the tall young man in their midst, who was talking to a cheeky little dog.

Some sort of negotiation appeared to be taking place. After a short while the young man turned to walk away. The little dog instantly began to trot along beside him, looking up now and then for a sign of approval. It was as if between canine nose and human heel were stretched a length of invisible elastic.

Nothing very remarkable about that, you might say; even the headstrong Beezle will stick by me for a minute or so if he thinks there could be a biscuit at the end of the ordeal. But what caught my attention was the gaze of pure astonishment on the face of a woman onlooker. It was plain she was the owner of the little dog. It was plainer still that never before in his whole scruffy life had he done anything so obliging as walk to heel.

Astonishment gave way to joy, and Dima had won himself two more fans. One was the dog, who continued to look at him adoringly after the training session was over; the other was the lady owner, who did likewise.

They were not alone. Dima Yeremenko and his Good Boy Dog School already seemed to have dozens of devotees in North London. I kept bumping into them. They would talk about Dima as if he were a magician, a guru, and there was some evidence of this. Whereas Beezle races off to filch picnickers' sandwiches, their dogs, at the command 'Down!', drop to their haunches in mid-gallop, as if shot. On the lead, their dogs promenade. Mine pulls like a husky hauling a sled across Alaska.

Then I began to notice copies of a jolly-looking newsletter lying about in the vet's waiting room. It contained stories about naughty dogs becoming angelic, savage terriers being converted to peace and love, reformed rescue dogs congratulated for their achievements. There were announcements about courses to be taken, including one called 'Well Trained or Clever? Advanced Communication Skills'.

This was the Good Boy Dog School magazine. It was circulating in Hendon, Hampstead, Highgate and Muswell Hill. It had more than 1,000 subscribers. And it was free. Evidently, something unusual was going on here.

I rang Dima on his mobile, having got his number from Issue 9 of the school mag. Could he give Beezle and me some training, please? We'd like to focus on walking to heel and sandwich-avoidance therapy. Yes, of course, Dima shouted, over a background noise of yaps, barks and heavy panting. But this was not a good week to arrange anything. The Good Boy Dog School was holding its annual summer boot camp in Norfolk, as I could probably hear. It was near King's Lynn. Maybe I would like to pay a visit?

Regretfully, I decided to leave Beezle behind. Since the only time I tried to get him into a mere lift he went as mad as a rodeo mustang, the prospect of a Tube and train journey was just too daunting.

It was a hot day. The Pentney Lakes Caravan Park regulars were sprawled in their camp-chairs reading the *Daily Mail*. I trudged along a sandy track for a couple of miles until I came across a far more animated scene: a small lakeside encampment of tents and trailers, in the midst of which sat or lay a circle of fourteen dogs, accompanied by about the same number of humans. The humans were wearing sunhats and taking notes. The dogs, while pretending to be cool and disengaged, were in fact paying close

attention to Dima, who was in the middle of the circle, teaching a Japanese Akita called Gem to jump over a low red and white fence.

At the third attempt, Gem, a big furry bitch with a strong personality and a curly tail, got the hang of it. Dima did nothing so crass as to show her what to do. He simply stood on the other side of the little jump and said 'Over' in a quiet voice. Gem realized something was required of her and that there would be what Dima called 'positive reinforcement', i.e. a tiny, liver-flavoured treat, if she guessed right.

After two botched sorties trying to go around the obstacle, she leapt over it instead – and got her biscuit, straight away. Reward must follow achievement instantaneously, Dima said. That way, the lesson would sink in. Dogs learn fast and forget slowly, which makes them eminently trainable. To demonstrate this to their sceptical owners, Dima had spent an hour or so the previous day teaching the dogs to press a red light switch with their noses. Incredibly, they all succeeded, including Snipe, the scatty Irish setter.

As a child, Dima's own dog was a setter. This was in Kharkov, in the Ukraine. The young Yeremenko was such a natural trainer that by the age of thirteen he had passed his first instructor's course, by fourteen he was part of a national display team and by nineteen had achieved the highest qualifications possible as both a trainer and a competition judge. To give all this dog-lore some academic backup, he took an MSc in the physiology of behaviour at Kharkov University, though he doesn't describe himself as a behaviourist.

'Clients are not so interested in *why* a dog has problems,' he says. 'They are interested in how to cure them. Owners want results, not reasons. I try to give them some of both.'

Dima came here six years ago. Apparently England has some of the best dog-trainers in the world – 'people who are legends back home'. At thirty-two, he seems to be rapidly approaching that status himself. We watched little Algy being instructed on how to sit up from a lying position, something his owner and he had not mastered. It took no more than two artful flicks of the lead, one liver treat and about thirty seconds before Algy was bouncing up and down down like a small, hairy yo-yo. A woman leaned over to me with shining eyes as we watched this performance. 'He's got the gift,' she said. 'We call him the dog-whisperer, you know.'

Dima doesn't do much whispering, as it happens. He strides about in his shorts and shades and ponytail, talking all the time with great fluency and an engaging Ukrainian accent. Words of wisdom come thick and fast.

'Always reinforce good behaviour.'

'Dogs must learn to enjoy being good.'

'If a dog's a fighter, reward him for making a decision *not* to fight. Even a pit bull can be trained to be completely docile.'

'If your dog steals shoes, here's what you do. At meal times you put down his bowl and a single shoe. He takes the shoe. You take away the bowl. After a day or two when he's had nothing to eat, he gets the message.'

It was time for agility. Dogs and humans strolled over to a field where a miniature gymkhana course was laid out over a length of about 80 yards. There were striped jumps and slalom poles and a curved plastic tunnel.

'This is the final chance to practise,' Dima announced. 'Tomorrow is the last day of camp and we have the big competition. The winner gets this magnificent trophy.' He pronounced the word to rhyme with 'toffee' and held up a three-inch statuette of a dog with its paw raised, mounted on a scarlet plastic plinth.

I surveyed the field dubiously. Apart from Gem, Algy and Snipe, there was Caspar the Battersea Dogs' Home lurcher, two pure-bred black Labradors and the impure, creamy-coloured Perrin, a whippet-Bedlington cross called Bedli, two dogs, Lily and Fred, who looked a bit like coyotes and had Inuit sled-dog in their genes, plus two bear-sized Leonbergers, Brenin and Astra, who would surely get stuck in the tunnel.

And there was Toby. Toby ambled over to lick my face. Close up, I couldn't help noticing he had only one eye. He looked a bit of a bruiser, type-cast for Bill Sikes's dog in *Oliver Twist*. John, his owner, seemed to be watching us with special anxiety as we made friends.

Then John said, 'Amazing, isn't it? When we came here on Monday I couldn't take him out without a muzzle on. He's a rescue dog. He'd fight anything in sight. Now look.'

I looked – and backed away a few inches from Toby's powerful jaws.

John was astounded and grateful at the change that had come over him in just four days. So was I.

To my surprise, the dogs went round the agility course not just with noisy enthusiasm but with some skill. Had they all been border collies it would have been like Cruft's. The big Leonbergers slid through the tunnel like ferrets, though Brenin refused at the third fence. Even one-eyed Toby trundled over the jumps with something approaching alacrity. It was extraordinary to behold. Beezle would have required a banquet of Gravybones to get him beyond the first hurdle.

Now it was one o'clock, time for the hand-feeding ceremony, to be done today with 'some simple heel-work-to-music exercises'. The dogs' bowls were laid out on a trestle table, piled with their lunchtime meals. Sandie, owner of the Leonbergers, backed up her Toyota 4WD and put on a disco tape with the volume up. Then each owner grabbed a handful of food. The idea was that instead of their usual free meal, the dogs would have to earn every mouthful of it. This happened twice a day.

Dima shouted instructions above the beat of the music. 'Three paces forward, three paces back!' 'Sit!' 'Roll over!' 'Paw!' 'Down!' 'About turn!' 'Heel!'

The dogs were fed a fistful of food only after each command was successfully obeyed. And, by golly, did they obey. Dogs and humans moved together in a frenzy of coordinated joy and anticipation. The scene was a cross between an aerobics class and a barn-dance. The final order was 'Speak!', at which all the dogs sat down and barked ecstatically, while the owners caught their breaths and clapped their hands.

Afterwards, we went for a walk by the river. There was a chaotic swimming race, in which two water-shy dogs took the plunge for the first time. Later came a mass walk-to-heel as we passed, first, a pair of swans with a family of cygnets, then a grass-snake or maybe it was an adder, basking in the shallows. The dogs were as disciplined as guardsmen. Dima, the pack-leader, walked in front. No dog was allowed to dominate.

Yet every dog, and its owner, was having a ball. *Homo sapiens* and his best friend were working and playing

together in a way I had never seen before. It was, quite simply, marvellous fun. How I wished Beezle had come along. He would have learned more in a day than I had taught him in a lifetime.

On the Heath a week later, I introduced him to Dima. They had a one-to-one discussion, covering sandwich-snatching and walking to heel. I can't say yet whether the encounter will change Beezle's life. But we shall be buying a tent and signing up for the next Good Boy Dog School boot camp.

It was baking hot this morning. Otherwise, it has been an indifferent summer, though that matters less than it would have if I didn't have a dog. I used to think I suffered from Seasonal Affective Disorder so acute that a grey day in August was as dashing to the spirits as a winter downpour. But walking a dog every day forces one to acknowledge the seasons and positively welcome nature's changing course untrimmed. How infernally dull to live in California, you come to think, where avocados are always cheap and the inhabitants must look to earthquakes and mudslides to relieve the tedium of eternal summer. How boring to have no outdoor gear but a pair of shorts and sandals. Here every change in the weather is a minor adventure for those who go out to meet it. Or so I tell myself, as I heave on the plastic trousers, pretending I am Ernest Shackleton, and trudge off once again into a drizzly dawn.

Actually, I do get a thrill from crunching over the frozen mud of Cohen's Field in January, when I will remember the cracked earth of this morning, the dog pushing through the tall grass like a prowling leopard, with his tongue lolling thirstily and the swifts skidding over his head. It is the same place, but utterly and miraculously different, just as it will be again in six months' time.

Tail Piece

At their best, dogs are catalysts. They affect our relationship with the world around us – mostly for the better, I think – without being changed themselves. If it were not for the familiar yet mysterious creature who at this very minute is butting me in the thigh, anticipating the chimes of Big Ben, which signal the six o'clock news for me and supper for him, I would not have been out on the Heath this morning.

I would not have spotted the heron, poised to seize his breakfast from beneath the opaque surface of his pond. I would not have seen the sun's first rays strike the vertical halo of the London Eye. I would have missed coming across a covey of film actors in top hats and Victorian capes, drinking tea out of styrofoam cups and dabbing their false moustaches, as though waiting to meet for a stroll around Kenwood with the somethingth Earl of Mansfield. Instead, I would have been at home in bed, or eating toast.

I would have missed the extreme pleasure of going for a walk with a good companion, who demonstrates with every step he takes and every wag of his tail his unreserved approval of the world around him.

'I asked nothing better of life. I still ask nothing better of life,' wrote Elizabeth von Arnim in her autobiography. 'These very things, just sun on my face, the feel of spring around the corner, and nobody anywhere in sight except a dog, are still enough to fill me with utter happiness. How convenient. And how cheap.'

Praise be to dog, I say blithely, then remember to collect a handful of poo-bags from the bundle by the gate. Aha. They have a new design on them, the silhouette of some sort of terrier with a pile of steaming dog-do beneath his tail. 'Clean it up!' the bag commands.

That rather puts things in perspective.

A Word from His Mistress

Valerie Grove writes:

When I was researching Dodie Smith's life, and wading through the millions of words in her self-obsessed diaries, I used to skip the scores of pages in which she rambled on about the exquisite beauty and charm of her successive Dalmatians, especially in the weeks of mourning after one of them had died. (Her seventh and last Dalmatian, Charley, outlived her, and died of a broken heart after she was taken away, at the age of ninety-four, from her cottage for the last time. He was buried by the gardener under the mulberry tree in the garden.)

But after eight and a half years with Beezle at the centre of our lives, it seems to me that The Man does not fully appreciate what The Dog represents in a household like ours.

Beezle's first great asset is his quite astonishing beauty. Being large and elegant and striking, he enhances the look of any room, stretched out on the sofa or alert at the window or obliterating the entire hearth. He can enfold himself into a furry circle, cocooned in cushions and pillows; a split-second later he is bounding up and leaping down several flights of stairs. Perhaps only a woman can eulogize his masculine muscularity, beguilingly combined with ermine softness of fur (especially under his chin) and silkiness of ears. The agility of his ears deserves a chapter to itself, their eloquence reflecting alertness, intent listening, relaxation, or eating-mode, when the ears become horizontal like wing-mirrors. So does the immense strength and resilience of his great paws with long, pale-pink fingernails. And a male creature who can pull one with ease up a steep hill, but will also lie on your bed on his back for hours, only wanting you to stroke his fur while he gazes up at you from black-linered brown eyes, must captivate the female heart.

Also, The Man does not mention the superiority of The Dog over The Child. The Dog will not reproach or defy you, wear absurd clothes found in charity shops or on skips, or criticize you for all your human failings. He is always there when you come home, manifestly thrilled to see you even if you have only been out to empty the dustbin for thirty seconds; and he stands patiently wagging while you search for your gloves, glasses, phone, before going out.

But I have to concede, since I observe it daily, that it is only for one person that Beezle will lie on the top stair, head dolefully between paws, staring at the front door when that person has gone out without him. And that is his Man.

Some Books About Dogs

Elizabeth von Arnim, *All the Dogs of My Life* (Virago Press, 1995)

Stephen Budiansky, *The Truth About Dogs* (Weidenfeld & Nicolson, 2001)

Jilly Cooper, *The Common Years* (Methuen, 1984)

Robert Drewe, *Walking Ella: A dog day dossier* (Box Press, 1998)

Elliott Erwitt, *Dogdogs* (Phaidon, 1998)

Roger Grenier (trans Alice Kaplan), *The Difficulty of Being a Dog* (University of Chicago Press, 2000)

Bud Johns (ed), *Old Dogs Remembered* (Carroll & Graf, 1993)

Elizabeth Marshall Thomas, *The Hidden Life of Dogs* (Weidenfeld & Nicolson, 1994)

The New Yorker Book of Dog Cartoons (Alfred A. Knopf, 1995)

Acknowledgements

The author and publisher wish to thank the following for permission to quote from copyright material: Faber & Faber Ltd for *Walking to School* in *Collected Poems*; Dutch Limited for the *A.A. Milne and Winnie-the-Pooh* and the extract of *Winnie-the-Pooh*, *I Pooh by Pooh Sticks* from *Pooh's Library*; W.W. Norton & Company; Faber & Faber; the Society of Authors as the Literary Representative of The National Trust for Places of Historic Interest or Natural Beauty; the Trustees of the National Library of Scotland; and Pearson Education for *The Book of Quotations*.

Acknowledgements

The author and publishers wish to thank the following for permission to quote from copyrighted material: Curtis Brown (Australia) Ltd for *Walking Ella* by Robert Drewe; Andre Deutsch Limited for 'For A Good Dog' by Ogden Nash; Executors of the estate of James MacGibbon for 'O Pug!' by Stevie Smith; George Sassoon for 'Man and Dog' by Siegfried Sassoon; Time Warner Books UK for *All the Dogs of My Life* by Elizabeth von Arnim; A.P. Watt Ltd on behalf of The National Trust for Places of Historical Interest or Natural Beauty, for 'Thy Servant A Dog' by Rudyard Kipling; A.P. Watt Ltd on behalf of the Royal Literary Fund for 'The Song of Quoodle' by G.K. Chesterton.